THE LEADERSHIP PAPERS

TOOLS FOR EFFECTIVE LEADERSHIP

Russell L. Davis

In Loving Memory
Gene and Peggy Vogelgesang

To God for His everlasting grace.
To my loving wife, Lori, for her patience and her smile.
To my friends and family.
Thank you for your constant support.

Our lives begin to end the day we become silent about things that matter. – Martin Luther King, Jr.

INTRODUCTION

For many years I facilitated workshops and wrote extensively on the concepts of race, values, behaviors, accountability, communication, and management, with a focus on leadership development. I believe that leadership is a key factor in personal and professional success.

Some believe that leadership is an exclusive characteristic reserved for the privileged or elite, connected to one's station in life, family name, education, or other measures of status.

I believe that leadership is inherent in everyone, but only those who practice and hone their skills become the best leaders.

True qualities of leadership are not predicated on wealth, class, race, gender, or position. They consist of intrinsic qualities connected to principled behaviors, personal responsibility, positive engagement, caring, and character.

> The supreme quality for leadership is unquestionably integrity. Without it, no real success is possible, no matter whether it is on a section gang, a football field, in an army, or in an office. – Dwight D. Eisenhower

During the 2016 presidential campaign, I was struck by the *lack* of personal responsibility and leadership demonstrated by many of the candidates, and penned an article titled, The Death of Responsibility:

> The presidential debates have ended, but the fallout from the statements and actions of the candidates and their surrogates may have a negative effect on the political process and civil discourse for years to come...
>
> Success in leadership is not achieved by standing on the necks of others or by destroying your reputation or the reputation of others, but by connecting with a set of positive guiding principles and working diligently in an ethical and positive manner to achieve results. Success and leadership require a dedication to responsible behavior that many of our 'successful leaders' lack.[i]

The behaviors of the candidates, their focus on insult and rudeness, was warping and undermining the fundamental ideals of leadership. I posed the question, "Is this the new normal, are we witnessing the death of personal responsibility?"

My concerns intensified after the election as the behaviors of the new administration deteriorated into bullying tactics, social and political divisiveness, "Alternative Facts," and a focus on winning at any cost.

Civility and respectful communication were discarded as a rejection of "political correctness."

> People who treat other people as less than human must not be surprised when the bread they have cast on the waters comes floating back to them, poisoned. – James A. Baldwin

The degradation of leadership continued with the pervasive allegations of sexual harassment and sexual abuse by those in positions of power: Bill Cosby, Harvey Weinstein, Kevin Spacey, Larry Nassar, Louis C.K, Al Franken, Stephen Wynn, Jerry Richardson, Andrea Ramsey, Eric Davis, Mario Batali, Trent Franks, Garrison Keillor, Matt Lauer, Charlie Rose, Danny Masterson, Brett Ratner, Michael Oreskes, Roy Moore, Roy Price, Andy Dick, Roger Ailes, Bill O'Reilly, Cristina Garcia, Tony Mendoza, and so many more. A 2018 National Study on Sexual Harassment and Assault found that 81% of Women and 43% of Men Have Experienced Sexual Abuse in [the] USA.[ii]

Politicians, entertainers, and *leaders* in industry believed their position, title, or station in life allowed them the right to act with impunity, completely disregarding the humanity of those they abused.

Why?

They confused power with leadership, tyranny with respect, dissent with treason, and partisanship with patriotism.

Time and time again individuals in *positions* of leadership were unable to display the *skills* of leadership. They were blinded by power and therefore blind to the responsibilities associated with power.

> Leadership is a privilege to better the lives of others. It is not an opportunity to satisfy personal greed. – Mwai Kibaki

As my faith in politicians, entertainers, and business leaders diminished, I was reminded of the words of Mahatma Gandhi, "You must not lose faith in humanity…"

I was encouraged by the rise in grassroots movements founded on principles of human dignity, transparency, inclusion, engagement, and speaking truth to power. The Women's March, Indivisible, Black Lives Matter, stopstreetharassment.org, Run for Something, #METOO, #ENOUGH, Take Back The Workplace, Sleeping Giants, March for Our Lives, and so many more; movements started by individuals motivated to engage in positive change.

> Leadership is not about a title or a designation. It's about impact, influence and inspiration… - Robin S. Sharma

Although there is tragedy, injustice, selfishness and heartbreak, there is also triumph, justice, selflessness, and joy. There are ordinary people willing to take a stand and demonstrate the essential skills of effective leadership.

> Anywhere, anytime ordinary people are given the chance to choose, the choice is the same: freedom, not tyranny; democracy, not dictatorship; the rule of law, not the rule of the secret police. – Tony Blair

The Leadership Papers was written to support individuals and organizations interested in engaging in leadership to create or sustain positive change.

> If we desire a society of peace, then we cannot achieve such a society through violence. If we desire a society without discrimination, then we must not discriminate against anyone in the process of building this society. If we desire a society that is democratic, then democracy must become a means as well as an end. – Bayard Rustin

Drawing on my experience as an executive, consultant, and trainer, I create a framework for understanding the roles, responsibilities, expectations, and challenges of leadership, and provide practical information on how to develop or enhance one's leadership skills.

I focus on the everyday leaders, those who influence others around them, whether they work in the mailroom or the boardroom. I share my philosophy on what is crucial in effective leadership, namely: values, integrity, vision, humility, effective communication, ethical decision making, respect, trustworthiness, understanding of self, understanding of others, understanding of the objective(s), practice, and patience.

The Leadership Papers includes conversations with leaders, articles, book reviews, definitions, quotes, tools for engagement, and information I have found helpful in my leadership development.

Whether you are just starting on your leadership journey or are a seasoned veteran, The Leadership Papers is designed to provide context for your continued growth and development.

Contents

- INTRODUCTION 7
- UNDERSTANDING LEADERSHIP 19
  - Leadership: A Tool To Achieve Success 19
    - Leadership Is Constantly Evolving 21
    - Key Lessons For Leaders 22
  - The Distinction Between Leadership And Supervision 24
  - Servant Leadership 28
    - Principles Of Servant Leadership Assessment 31
  - The 5-Core Skills Of Exceptional Leaders 32
  - Successful Continuous Development (SCD) 35
  - Leadership In Action: Ethical Decision Making, Customer Service, Innovation, And Integrity 38
    - Customer Service: A Critical Function Of Leadership 39
    - The Importance Of Innovation 41
    - Integrity: The Foundation Of Leadership, Individual, And Organizational Success 44
- LEADERSHIP COMMUNICATION 53
  - Effective Communication 53
    - Hot Buttons 56
    - The TDC Communication Exercise 57
    - Communication Exercise Worksheet 60
  - Dialogue, A Key To Understanding 61
    - The Role Of Dialogue 65
    - Why Dialogue? 66
    - Nine (9) Essential Skills For Facilitation 67
  - Behavior in leadership: "Behavior Breeds Behavior" 71
  - Practicing Personal Accountability With The QBQ!® 73
    - Behavior And Personal Accountability: A Partnership For Success 76
  - Effectively Addressing The Elephant In The Room 78

DISTINCTIVE QUALITIES OF LEADERS ... 85

- Leaders Are Trustworthy ... 85
  - Characteristics Of Trustworthiness ... 88
- Leaders Are Ethical ... 89
- Leaders Are Thankful ... 91
- Leaders Are Hopeful ... 93
- Leaders Are Dreamers ... 95
- Leaders Listen And Provide Actionable Advice ... 97
- Leaders Provide Motivation ... 100
- Leaders Must Raise The Bar On Personal Accountability Or Face The Death Of Responsibility ... 104
- Leaders Maintain Perspective Through Tough Times ... 108
- Leaders Recognize The Impact Of Their Choices ... 111
- Leaders Demonstrate Commitment ... 114
- Leaders Recognize The Importance Of Developing Relationships ... 116
- Leaders Do Not Fear Change ... 118
- Leaders Control The First Move And Intend To Engage Meaningfully ... 121
- Leaders Recognize The Value Of Team ... 123
- Leaders Have Fun ... 126
- Leaders Do Not Need A Crystal Ball To Predict The Future ... 129
- Leaders Actively Engage In Problem Solving ... 132
- Leaders Move From "Why Me?" To "Now What?" ... 134
- Leaders Know The Magic Number ... 136
- Leaders Resolve Conflict ... 139
- Leaders Recognize The Difference Between Being A "Boss" And Being A "Leader" ... 143
- Leaders Have A Spirit Of Renewal And Happiness ... 147

THE LEADERSHIP PAPERS INTERVIEWS ... 153

- Jane Camarillo, Ph.D. ... 154
- Phil Clement ... 160

Sarah Goldstein Herman, Esq. 166
Jana Hunter 170
Alan Jenkins, Esq. 175
John P. Keil, Esq. 178
Niloufer Pabla 185
Sukhi S. Pabla 188
Lucille Renwick 192
John Ridley 195
Ida Shum, Esq. 205
Tina Zee 208
ACKNOWLEDGMENTS 213
INDEX 216
ENDNOTES 218

CHAPTER ONE

UNDERSTANDING LEADERSHIP

A leader is a dealer in hope. — Napoleon Bonaparte

UNDERSTANDING LEADERSHIP

Leadership: A Tool To Achieve Success

What is leadership?

Webster's Dictionary defines leadership as:

> The power or ability to lead other people.[iii]

This traditional definition of leadership is connected to an outdated understanding of what it means to lead. To many, leadership is inextricably tied to power, and powerful leaders *win at all costs*. This Machiavellian perspective ignores key values of leadership and focuses solely on the outcome(s) and not the journey.

I see leadership as much more than "The *power* or ability to lead other people." It is a *way of being*, a preparedness, a process that drives actions and directs behaviors. At its essence:

> Leadership is a tool to achieve success.

If one understands leadership as a *tool*, then, as with all tools, mastery comes from practice, care, and responsible use.

Effective leadership requires a commitment to key values demonstrated through behaviors. The key values of leadership are accountability, character, effective communication, understanding of self, understanding of others, understanding of the objective(s), practice, and patience.

With *practice*, *care*, and *responsible use*, the *tool* of leadership leads to success.

Webster's Dictionary defines success as:

> The fact of getting or achieving wealth, respect, or fame.[iv]

In today's toxic business and political environments, for some, success means winning at all costs while exploiting relationships and destroying reputations.

The *traditional*, pull-yourself-up-by-your-bootstraps-rugged-individualism-win-at-all-cost-take-no-prisoners view of success is flawed and does not reward or acknowledge the broader more attainable idea of success – an idea based on inclusion, shared values, and common goals. Success should not be defined solely by superstars, but by ordinary people working together to make a positive impact on those around them.

These *traditional* definitions of leadership and success are *technically* correct, but they do not address the importance of *how* one achieves success or demonstrates leadership.

I propose an update to these definitions:

- Leadership – The ability to effectively and responsibly engage with people, processes, and programs, to achieve organizational, team, or individual goals.
- Success – Attaining your dreams while maintaining your dignity.

This new definition of leadership enhances the traditional version by requiring a leader to demonstrate responsibility and engagement with those she leads. The updated meaning of success supports Webster's definition but adds the guiding principle of *maintaining your dignity,* as you achieve your dreams.

Nowhere in these new definitions is there a suggestion that leaders should shy away from challenges, have a meek, milquetoast, hat-in-hand attitude or lose all drive, competitive spirit, or the will to be the best. These enhancements simply provide a compass for the journey.

Attaining success, or fulfilling your dreams, demands that you fight and struggle and practice and work and fail before you succeed, but you achieve *your idea* of success with your dignity intact and without destroying relationships.

Effectively and responsibly engaging others - not destroying, demeaning, or castigating others to do your will - is a cornerstone of the new leadership model.

Take a closer look at your personal definitions of success and leadership. Are they focused solely on the end goal regardless of the impact on you and others, or are you paying attention to the effect you have as you travel the road to achieving your dreams?

Leadership Is Constantly Evolving

As societies evolve, as new technologies are developed, as values shift and new understandings of the needs and wants of individuals change, effective leaders adapt to ensure that they are engaging with people <u>where they are</u>, not demanding that others abandon their values and conform to the ideals of the leader.

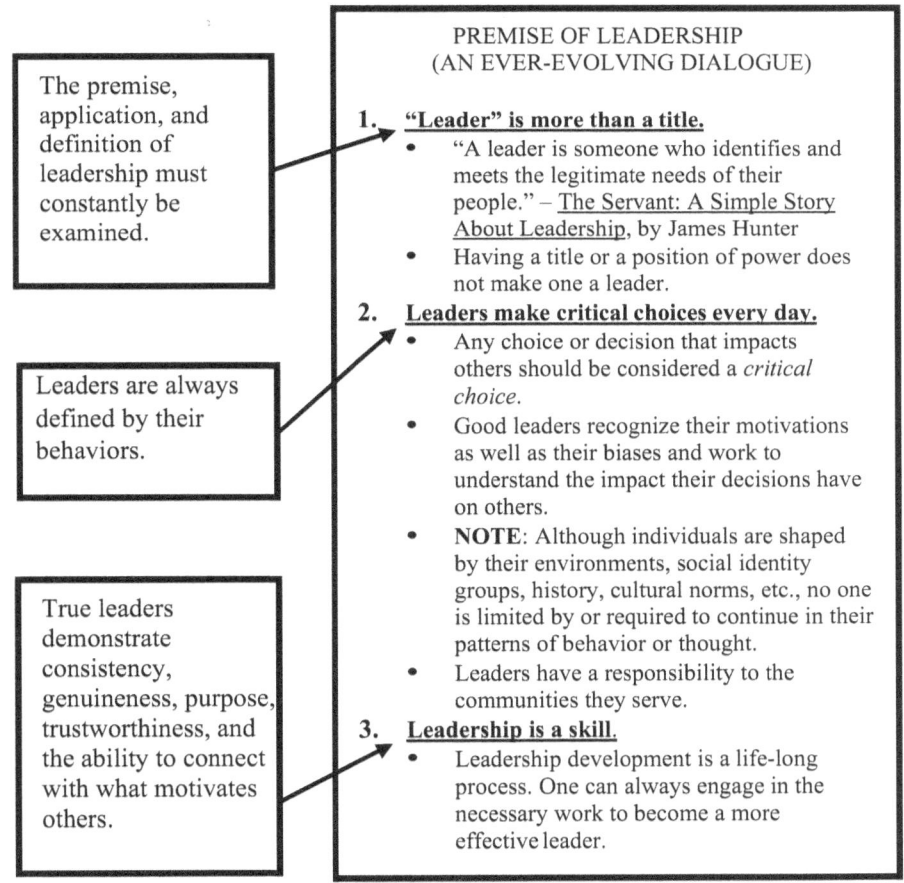

Leadership is not about force or control, it is about understanding that all individuals have a choice in how they act, including who they follow.

The most effective leaders recognize that leadership always requires sacrifice and service to the cause, mission, vision, and the people being served. If the sacrifice is perceived as genuine, leaders are rewarded with trust and respect, creating dedicated, committed, and motivated supporters.

Leaders make critical decisions every day. *Successful* leaders recognize that any decision that impacts another person is considered critical.

Leadership requires the gathering of facts, not just opinions, developing a deep understanding of process, cultivating courage, and learning the skill of effective execution (as described in chapter three). Successful leaders solicit input from multiple sources. They execute with as much information and understanding of potential outcomes as possible.

A leader's behavior, how they engage with others, navigate difficulty, recover from mistakes, etc., the choices the leader makes define whether they deserve and/or receive support.

Key Lessons For Leaders

Effective leadership does not require perfection – leaders are as imperfect as the next person, but how the leader works, communicates, and recovers from mistakes determines if they gain, maintain, or lose respect and trust.

Leaders are always under scrutiny and will constantly be tested – this fact should not deter or overwhelm leaders. It should serve as a catalyst for positive, meaningful, and intentional behaviors. Successful leaders consistently live by their values but are also open to discovery and growth.

Leaders are like batteries – those around you draw from you as if you were a power source. They draw on your encouragement, strength, compassion, understanding, honesty, courage, and demonstrated humanity. One of the greatest challenges in leadership is learning how to effectively recharge your batteries so that you can continue to offer support to others without becoming so drained that you lose your ability to lead. It is imperative that leaders engage in self-care.

> Self-care is any activity that we do deliberately in order to take care of our mental, emotional, and physical health. Although it's a simple concept in theory, it's something we very often overlook. Good self-care is key to improved mood and reduced anxiety. It's also key to a good relationship with oneself and others.[v] - Raphailia Michael, MA

<u>Success and leadership go hand in hand</u> - how one achieves success and how one demonstrates leadership is determined by the hands they hold and the moral compass that guides them along the way.

Leadership, the <u>ability</u> to <u>effectively</u> and <u>responsibly</u> <u>engage</u> with people, processes, and programs, to achieve organizational, team, or individual <u>goals</u>.

This definition highlights five (5) qualities of leadership:

- **Ability** - Skill
- **Effectiveness** - Success
- **Responsibility** - Trustworthiness
- **Engagement** - Behavior
- **Goal Achievement** - Execution

These five (5) qualities are interwoven throughout The Leadership Papers and serve as the foundation of the book. Mastery of these qualities requires individuals to cultivate compassion, courage, conviction, and purpose in their leadership role. Doing so will strengthen interactions, foster a commitment to excellence, enhance relationships, and ultimately make one a more effective leader.

Too often we underestimate the power of a touch, a smile, a kind word, a listening ear, an honest compliment, or the smallest act of caring, all of which have the potential to turn a life around. – Leo Buscaglia

The Distinction Between Leadership And Supervision

The terms supervision and leadership are often used interchangeably, but they are two unique activities engaged in to achieve specific outcomes.

> <u>Supervision</u> is the activity carried out by supervisors to oversee the productivity and progress of employees who report directly to them. Supervision is a management activity and supervisors have a management role in the organization.[vi]
>
> <u>Leadership</u> is the ability to effectively and responsibly engage with people, processes, and programs, to achieve organizational, team, or individual goals.

Within both definitions there is a desire for a specific outcome, typically task completion. There is also an implicit desire for the task to be completed meeting stated or desired guidelines, specifications, and expectations of the organization, department, unit, client, etc.

Many supervision models focus on task completion and *end results* and use leadership as one *technique* to reach goals or objectives. I believe there should be a focus on leadership as the primary process to meet organizational needs and objectives.

The core or fundamental skills of supervision *can* also be attributes of leadership *when applied appropriately*. We are addressing supervision from a leadership perspective which moves from **management**, which often focuses solely on the end results, to **leadership**, which focuses as much on the people and the process as it does on the outcome.

Our leadership/supervision framework focuses on creating personal connections to meet individual and organizational goals.

Why focus on leadership?

A leader is interpreted as someone who sets direction in an effort to influence people to follow their direction. They set direction by developing a clear vision and mission, and conducting planning that determines the goals needed to achieve the vision and mission. They motivate by using a variety of methods, including facilitation, coaching, mentoring, directing, delegating, etc.[vii]

One of the key functions of management is leading along with planning, organizing and controlling. Leaders carry out their roles in a wide variety of styles, e.g., autocratic, democratic, participatory, laissez-faire (hands off), etc. Often, the leadership style depends on the situation, including the life cycle of the organization.[viii]

Regardless of style, good leaders and good supervisors should cultivate the skills represented in the **C.A.R.E.S. Model.**

Communication – Open, honest, direct, and appropriate communication is critical for successful interactions. Providing opportunities for input and feedback, sharing ideas, discussing goals, and demonstrating a willingness to listen, contributes to the creation of a community where great ideas are brought forward to support individual and organizational success.

- Supervisors/leaders must set clear expectations as to what effective communication means for them and their teams.

Accountability – Taking personal responsibility for your actions, being accessible and present in your interactions, and being approachable to your colleagues and clients.

- Supervisors/leaders must ensure that their employees/staff have the necessary skills to complete the tasks.

Responsibility – Recognizing that you have the power to impact others – positively or negatively. Each person serves as the face of their team or organization, and their individual actions support or undermine the values of the organization. Responsibility means demonstrating courage and making the choice to do what is right.

- Supervisors/leaders must provide appropriate information, including incentives and consequences, to help staff succeed. This requires an understanding of the motivations of the members of your team(s).

Engagement – Connecting appropriately with individuals and teams to foster positive relationships. Commit to understanding the history, organizational culture, values, challenges, needs, wants, etc., necessary to create a positive environment.

- Supervisors/leaders must interact constructively with colleagues and staff at all levels and demonstrate a willingness to be helpful.

Service – Willingly providing your time and talents for the success of the organization. Regardless of position or title, we all can serve as leaders. Collaborative action for good is the essence of true leadership.

- Participate fully to support the success of your teams, colleagues, and the organization.

Focusing solely on outcomes or task completion does not make a person an effective supervisor or an effective leader. The C.A.R.E.S. Model highlights the importance of positive interpersonal behaviors to meet organizational and team needs.

Leaders must also *demonstrate* caring. The **CARI(ng)® Process** supplements the C.A.R.E.S. Model with practical techniques that are person-centered and unambiguous. The **CARI(ng)® Process** promotes **C**lear Expectations, **A**ppropriate Skill, **R**ewards, and **I**ncentives.

Clear expectations – Set clear expectations and provide consistent direction. Ensure that organizational, departmental, supervisory, and task completion expectations are clear.

Appropriate skill – Ensure that your team members have the necessary skills to complete the assigned tasks and that you have the necessary skills to support your team. Participate in life-long learning and commit to personal and professional development.

Rewards – Provide the appropriate rewards to continuously support the needs of the members of your team. Rewards are either financial or relational and are most effective when you understand what the individual needs to succeed as well as what you and the organization **can** and **will** provide to support that success.

Incentives – Provide appropriate incentives to help your team succeed. This requires an understanding of the motivations of the members of your team as well as an understanding of the objectives and expectations of the task, project, or position. Be clear about the objectives, expectations, and the consequences. A consequence is different from a threat, it is simply an outcome resulting from an action. Communicating the potential positive and negative outcomes is critical to establishing understanding and/or acceptance.

There are many pathways to gaining skills as a supervisor, but **CARI(ng)®** about others is crucial to leadership development.

As with any model, there are additional skills, tools, and nuances necessary for successful execution, e.g., caring for the individual, caring for the team, recognizing your strengths and weaknesses, honestly and consistently evaluating your performance and growth, knowledge of what is needed to inspire, connect with, and understand others, etc. But to be most effective using the **CARI(ng)®** Process, one must develop the 5-Core Skills Of Exceptional Leaders, discussed later in this chapter. Honing these skills will enhance your leadership ability and create a pathway to successful engagement with your teams.

Leadership is not about titles, positions, or flowcharts. It is about one life influencing another. — John C. Maxwell

Servant Leadership

Servant leadership refers to:

> A method of development for leaders originally advanced by authors Peter Block and Robert Greenleaf. Servant leadership stresses the importance of the role a leader plays as the steward of the resources of a business or other organization, and teaches leaders to serve others while still achieving the goals set forth by the business.[ix]

The ideals of servant leadership are timeless. They are rooted in a set of principles, ideals, and values that allow individuals to give of themselves unselfishly to strengthen the skills, abilities, and well-being of others. In servant leadership you give of yourself, not because of who the others are; you give because of who you are.

The phrase "servant leadership" was first published by Robert Greenleaf in an article in 1970, entitled <u>The Servant as Leader</u>. Greenleaf made several statements on the difference in motivations between the "leader-first" perspective and the "servant-first" perspective.

> The servant-leader is servant first... It begins with the natural feeling that one wants to serve, to serve first. Then conscious choice brings one to aspire to lead. That person is sharply different from one who is leader first, perhaps because of the need to assuage an unusual power drive or to acquire material possessions... The leader-first and the servant-first are two extreme types. Between them there are shadings and blends that are part of the infinite variety of human nature.
>
> The difference manifests itself in the care taken by the servant-first to make sure that other people's highest priority needs are being served. The best test, and difficult to administer, is: Do those served grow as persons? Do they, while being served, become healthier, wiser, freer, more autonomous, more likely themselves to become servants? And, what is the effect on the least privileged in society? Will they benefit or at least not be further deprived?[x]

While the ideals of servant leadership may be timeless, understanding how to apply the key principles to our daily lives can be a challenge. In his book, The Servant: A Simple Story About Leadership, James Hunter weaves these principles into a story, allowing the readers to see the ideas as practical, applicable, and attainable.

If you have read the book, I encourage you to read it again. Each reading allows for a deeper understanding and a better sense of how to apply the principles to one's own life. For those who have not read The Servant, I encourage you to do so, as it can transform your personal and professional relationships.

The following overview of James Hunter's book highlights several key concepts:

The Servant: A Simple Story About Leadership, by James Hunter

- Leadership – the *skill* of *influencing people* to work enthusiastically towards goals identified as being for the common good.[xi]
- Leadership is about getting things done through people.[xii]
- The key to leadership is accomplishing the task at hand while building relationships.[xiii]
- A leader is someone who identifies and meets the legitimate needs of their people – NEEDS, not wants.
  - A want is simply a wish or desire without any regard for the physical or psychological consequences.
  - A need is a legitimate physical and/or psychological requirement for the well-being of a human being.[xiv]

How do you learn the needs of others? Ask. Constantly. Once you have gathered information on the needs of others you must choose to act. Align feelings with actions and treat people with value and respect.

$$\text{Intentions} - \text{actions} = \text{squat}^{xv}$$
$$\text{Intentions} + \text{actions} = \text{will}^{xvi}$$

Leadership is not about personality, possessions, or charisma, but all about who you are as a person. Leadership is not about style; it is about substance, namely, character.[xvii]

> **Principles of Servant Leadership:**
> - **Patience** – Showing Self-Control
> - **Kindness** – Giving Attention, Appreciation, and Encouragement
> - **Humility** – Being Authentic and Without Pretense or Arrogance
> - **Respectfulness** – Treating Others as Important People
> - **Selflessness** – Meeting the Needs of Others
> - **Forgiveness** – Giving Up Resentment when Wronged
> - **Honesty** – Being Free from Deception
> - **Commitment** – Sticking to Your Choices
> - **Resulting in service and sacrifice. Also resulting in TRUST. TRUST COMES FROM BEING TRUSTWORTHY.**

[xviii]

Thoughts become actions, actions become habits, habits become our character, and our character becomes our destiny.[xix]

The Servant provides valuable lessons on engagement and admonishes leaders to treat people as their greatest resource. It teaches that those with the responsibility to work with others should focus on *leadership* as opposed to *management* and operate from a position of *authority* as opposed to *power*.

- Manage – 1: to handle or direct with a degree of skill, 2: to succeed in accomplishing, 3: to achieve one's purpose. 4: to organize things in a formal, structured manner. [xx]
- Leadership – the skill of influencing people to work enthusiastically towards goals identified as being for the common good. [xxi]
- Power – the ability to force or coerce someone to do your will, even if they would choose not to, because of your position or your might. [xxii]
- Authority – the skill of getting people to willingly do your will because of your personal influence. [xxiii]

To achieve organizational success, leaders should adopt a Person-Centric Perspective. This requires a shift from *management*, with a focus on power, to *authority*, with a focus on leadership to drive workflow, outcomes, and interactions.

Successful leaders understand the mission, vision, values, and goals of the organization and focus on those core ideals in every interaction.

In addition, servant leaders understand their ongoing journey to develop the core principles of servant leadership and work to bridge the gaps between their rhetoric and their behaviors.

Principles Of Servant Leadership Assessment

On a scale from 1 to 6, rate yourself on the frequency with which you demonstrate or display the Principles of Servant Leadership.

1. Place an "**X**" in the column for each principle describing your <u>typically demonstrated behavior</u>. **Note**: Choose the context for the exercise: at work, with family, friends, etc.

Principles	Almost never					Very often
Patience	1	2	3	4	5	6
Kindness	1	2	3	4	5	6
Humility	1	2	3	4	5	6
Respectfulness	1	2	3	4	5	6
Selflessness	1	2	3	4	5	6
Forgiveness	1	2	3	4	5	6
Honesty	1	2	3	4	5	6
Commitment	1	2	3	4	5	6
Service/sacrifice	1	2	3	4	5	6

2. Circle a number for your <u>desired behavior</u> for each word.
3. Circle the <u>principles</u> with the greatest separation between your <u>typically demonstrated behavior</u> and your <u>desired behavior.</u>
4. Choose two (2) principles that you will commit to improve.

1. _____   2. _____

If your actions inspire others to dream more, learn more, do more and become more, you are a leader.
— John Quincy Adams

The 5-Core Skills Of Exceptional Leaders

There are many styles, traits, and philosophies leaders can engage in to achieve their goals, but I believe there are 5-core skills that all exceptional leaders share.

First, let us differentiate between a leadership style, trait, or philosophy and a leadership *skill*.

- Style – a particular way in which something is done, created, or performed. [xxiv]
- Trait – a distinguishing quality (as of personal character) *b*: an inherited characteristic. [xxv]
- Philosophy – a particular set of ideas about knowledge, truth, the nature and meaning of life, etc. *b*: a set of ideas about how to do something or how to live. [xxvi]

A leader's style, trait(s), or philosophy, is based on a set of beliefs, values, and experiences, that may include cultural and environmental factors as driving forces in a leader's behavior.

- Skill – proficiency, facility, or dexterity that is acquired or developed through training or experience. [xxvii]

Simply put, a skill is an ability that has been acquired through training. A leader can choose any number of styles to achieve their goals, e.g., autocratic, democratic, participatory, laissez-faire, etc., and their choices often depend on temperament, personality, circumstance, and the needs of the organization or team being led. There are also numerous models or philosophies of leadership that one can follow, e.g., servant leader, democratic leader, principle-centered leader, visionary leader, total leader, etc., to reach desired goals. Regardless of style, traits, or philosophy, an individual must *develop* the skills necessary to become a good leader.

All good leaders engage in some type of training or practice to develop their leadership skills, but exceptional leaders develop and enhance 5-core skills:

1. Understanding of self
2. Understanding of others
3. Understanding of the objective(s)
4. Practice
5. Patience

Honing these skills allows leaders to master techniques that transcend styles, traits, and philosophies, and display qualities of leadership that inspire others to reach their goals.

1. <u>Understanding of self</u> – requires an intimate and honest recognition of strengths and weaknesses, and the courage or will to engage in self-improvement. Exceptional leaders do not settle for the, "I am what I am," philosophy. They work to become who they want to be. Fate does not create exceptional leaders; will, understanding, and appropriate action make exceptional leaders. Understanding of self requires Successful Continuous Development (SCD).

2. <u>Understanding of others</u> – requires a recognition and acknowledgement of the importance of the "other." It requires moving past the fear of difference and learning what is needed to motivate, inspire, connect-with and engage-with others. This idea is crucial to accomplishing shared goals and requires SCD.

    - Understanding of others requires one to engage with different views, people, cultures, values, etc., with a genuine desire to learn about difference – not to exploit the difference – but to *engage* with difference.
    - Understanding of others does not require a change in personal beliefs or values but does require a genuine desire to understand and move past assumptions.

3. <u>Understanding of the objective(s)</u> – requires clarity of the desired or expected outcome. This allows a committed leader to seek out the best resources necessary to achieve success and reach their goals.

4. <u>Practice</u> – requires repetition. We often forget that practice, doing what it takes to hone our skills, again, and again, and again, is crucial to skills development. Practice creates muscle memory, the ability for the body and mind to reflexively engage in the desired behavior. With practice and repetition, actions become seamless. To develop *Leadership Muscle Memory*, one must practice until values are demonstrated in behaviors. Practice makes behaviors permanent. .

5. <u>Patience</u> – requires self-control and executive function. All great achievements take time, but managing our responses to time, demonstrating self-control, and mastering our cognitive and behavioral responses are necessary components of patience. Cultivating patience allows for the development of perspective, knowledge, and ultimately wisdom.

Becoming an exceptional leader takes time, dedication, and courage. Mastering these 5-core skills, *Understanding of self, Understanding of others, Understanding of the objective(s), Practice,* and *Patience*, can lead to greater personal and professional fulfillment, more effective management, more engaged relationships, and demonstrate a commitment to ethical leadership.

You cannot hope to build a better world without improving the individuals. To that end, each of us must work for his own improvement and, at the same time, share a general responsibility for all humanity, our particular duty being to aid those to whom we think we can be most useful. — Marie Curie

Successful Continuous Development (SCD)

SCD refers to the deliberate or intentional actions a leader engages in to support the skills of <u>understanding self</u> and <u>understanding others</u>.

SCD consists of the following:

1. Enhancing communication skills
2. Engaging in continuous learning, formally and informally
3. Developing emotional intelligence
4. Cultivating genuineness
5. Being accountable

The world is a diverse place, with a multiplicity of thoughts, actions, needs, wants, communication styles, technologies, learning models, opportunities, events, etc. Responsible leaders recognize that they may be leading diverse teams with cultures, customs, values, beliefs, and experiences very different from their own, and work to create cohesion, <u>not</u> conformity.

SCD allows leaders to stay contemporary, relevant, and able to engage with others. This does not mean that leaders need to become experts on all topics, fads, technologies, cultures, etc. It means that they develop the ability to remain open to different ideas without reflexively rejecting alternate views, putting up walls, treating difference as inferior, or dismissing new or alternative views as a matter of principle. It requires emotional and intellectual honesty and is supported by Appreciative Inquiry (AI):

> Appreciative Inquiry is the cooperative search for the best in people, their organizations, and the world around them. It involves systematic discovery of what gives a system 'life' when it is most effective and

> capable in economic, ecological, and human terms. AI involves the art and practice of asking questions that strengthen a system's capacity to heighten positive potential. It mobilizes inquiry through crafting an 'unconditional positive question' often involving hundreds or sometimes thousands of people.[xxviii] – David Cooperrider and Diana Whitney

Successful leaders see the world with eyes open to opportunity, not closed and shuttered by fear, inflexibility of doctrine, policy, culture, belief, assumptions, stereotypes, prejudice, or difference.

> Too often, we judge other groups by their worst examples, while judging ourselves by our own best intentions. – President George W. Bush

SCD is a process of *paying attention* or *being present* that encourages personal accountability through 5-key actions:

1. Enhancing Communication Skills – developing clear and effective communication in written and spoken form, developing effective presentation skills, learning the skills of dialogue as opposed to debate, and mastering the 9 skills of facilitation:
    1. Validating someone's experience
    2. Listening without judgment - bracketing judgments
    3. Synthesizing information
    4. Helping someone rephrase a question/statement for clarity and understanding
    5. Asking questions without bringing in judgments
    6. Identifying and challenging assumptions
    7. Challenging a statement without de-valuing the person
    8. Providing information/teaching while maintaining collegiality (peership)
    9. Recognizing the teachable moments

    (Core skills training developed by The Dialogue Consultants)

2. Engaging In Continuous Learning – ongoing formal education, certificate or extension programs, reading for knowledge and understanding, engaging in personal assessments, e.g., MBTI, DiSC® Assessments, Coaching, etc. Developing servant leadership skills, volunteering with organizations to connect with others and understand difference.

   NOTE: connecting or engaging with diverse communities should be non-exploitive. Engagement must be genuine and undertaken to develop awareness, empathy, gratitude, understanding, and learning.

3. Developing Emotional Intelligence – "The capacity to be aware of, control, and express one's emotions, and to handle interpersonal relationships judiciously and empathetically."[xxix]

   Emotional intelligence (EI) is the capability of individuals to recognize their own and other people's emotions, discern between different feelings and label them appropriately, use emotional information to guide thinking and behavior, and manage and/or adjust emotions to adapt to environments or achieve one's goal(s).[xxx]

4. Cultivating Genuineness – Endeavor to be free from pretense or hypocrisy. Be sincere. Learn about your inherent biases and act to change your behaviors.

5. Being Accountable – "A personal choice to rise above one's circumstances and demonstrate the ownership necessary for achieving Key Results; to See It,® Own It,® Solve It,® and Do It.®"[xxxi] – The Oz Principle®

SCD provides opportunities to learn about our emotional and intellectual "triggers," control instinctual reactions and responses, align our values with our behaviors, and be present and engaged in more meaningful ways. SCD allows individuals to fully participate in their responsibilities as leaders and can allow for more honest and genuine relationships.

Leadership and learning are indispensable to each other. – John F. Kennedy

> *Ethics must begin at the top of an organization. It is a leadership issue and the chief executive must set the example.* — Edward Hennessy

Leadership In Action: Ethical Decision Making, Customer Service, Innovation, And Integrity

In his book, What the CEO Wants You to Know: How Your Company Really Works, Ram Charan states that a company achieves success when, "Their growth is profitable, sustainable, and capital efficient."

Profitability, Sustainability, and Capital Efficiency are important, but leaders must also integrate three additional components to achieve organizational success and demonstrate *Leadership in Action*:

- Customer Service
- Innovation
- Integrity

These are not simply lofty ideals, they are real, attainable, concrete goals, connected to a specific set of actions.

- Customer Service is a set of behaviors that demonstrate to clients – internal and external – that they are important, appreciated and valued.
- Innovation means introducing or creating something new and *valuable*. Innovation is not limited to technology, it includes how we think, how we work through adversity, and how we act when solving problems. It requires that we keep a fresh and open approach to all that we do.
- Integrity means having moral strength, completeness, or soundness. It is the foundation on which customer service and innovation are built.

All three ideals are *demonstrated* through behaviors. Although organizations are not *required* to demonstrate integrity as a condition of financial success, leaders should recognize that many consumers and clients support organizations based on their shared values. Leaders must recognize that companies, just like people, should do the "right" thing, not just what is the most profitable.

Leaders should promote Customer Service, Innovation, and Integrity as fundamental business and engagement practices.

The following essays will offer suggestions and support on how to integrate these principles into your leadership routine.

> *It is not blindly pushing your own agenda that will really create rich opportunities in your life, career, business – and in the world. It's is your ability to understand, appreciate, anticipate, address, add value to that of others that will.* – Rasheed Ogunlaru

Customer Service: A Critical Function Of Leadership

Customer Service is a phrase we hear often, but do leaders understand what it really means to provide customer service?

Jack Speer defines excellent customer service as:

> ... the process by which your organization delivers its services or products in a way that allows the customer to access them in the most efficient, fair, cost effective, and humanly satisfying and pleasurable manner possible.

The key to this definition is the phrase:

> *"...humanly satisfying and pleasurable..."*

Customer service requires making the customer <u>feel</u> appreciated by meeting their needs. There is no magic formula to address all client needs, but the components of successful customer service include treating the client as *they* want to be treated, being attentive and respectful during the interaction, and demonstrated knowledge of the service or product.

I recommend the Triple A's of Customer Service for meeting client needs.

> **Triple A's of Customer Service:**
>
> **Approachable, Available, Accountable**
>
> 1. All staff members will be <u>approachable.</u>
> 2. All staff members will be <u>available.</u>
> 3. All staff members will be <u>accountable.</u>

Being approachable requires one to be present, engaging, and attentive in whatever form the interaction takes place – in person, over the phone, chat line, etc. Engaging with a detached, uninterested, or distracted staff member undermines interactions and spoils the customer experience.

Being available is imperative to the transaction. Regardless of how approachable an individual is, it will not matter if they cannot be reached by clients when needed.

Being accountable requires self-awareness. It requires one to choose to behave in an appropriate manner to foster positive interactions. Choosing to be accountable motivates individuals to gain a mastery of the product or service they represent and to take appropriate actions to address problems.

In our technologically savvy society, clients also expect e-commerce systems to be approachable, available, and accountable to facilitate a rich customer experience. Having a complicated e-commerce portal, online or mobile systems that have unwieldy navigation, poor content and product descriptions, digital payment failures, delivery and logistics problems, or poor security, will frustrate your customers and undermine your online reputation and ROI.

In the book <u>Delivering Knock Your Socks Off Service</u>, by Performance Research Associates, total customer service is evaluated using five steps:

1. <u>Reliability</u> – the ability to provide what is promised dependably and accurately.
2. <u>Assurance</u> – the knowledge and courtesy you show to customers, and your ability to convey trust, competence and confidence.
3. <u>Tangibles</u> – the physical facilities and equipment, your own - and other's appearance.
4. <u>Empathy</u> – the degree of caring and individual attention you show customers.
5. <u>Responsiveness</u> – the willingness to help customers promptly.[xxxii]

These five actions are considered essential to meeting client needs.

The ability or choice to provide quality customer service can make or break an organization, so much so that the International Customer Service Association (ICSA) has a vision to "…advance awareness of the importance of customer service within organizations, and position Service Professionals as THE MOST vital element of any organizations growth strategies."[xxxiii]

Providing excellent customer service should be a cornerstone of every company's mission statement, demonstrated through reliability, assurance, tangibles, empathy, and responsiveness.

The website Customer Service Point, in an article titled A Different Customer Service Definition, discusses three concepts of service:

1. Customer Service is a function of how well an organization meets the needs of its customers.
2. Customer Service is a function of how well an organization is able to constantly and consistently exceed the needs of the customer.
3. A customer defines good customer service as how she perceives that an organization has delighted her, by exceeding to meet her needs.

Customer service is more than just completing a set of tasks; it is about understanding the *perceptions* and *feelings* of the client as the service or task was being completed. Did they feel confident in your ability, listened to, understood, in addition to receiving the service that they expected?

Successful leaders and organizations listen to their clients' needs, deliver on their promises, and succeed.

> *We cannot solve our problems with the same thinking we used when we created them.* – Albert Einstein

The Importance Of Innovation

Successful leaders and businesses need to be deliberate, skillful, and agile enough to maneuver in their chosen markets. They must follow the tried and true axiom, "adapt or die."

Adaptation is crucial for survival.

Many companies do not adapt, or they adapt too slowly and are one step behind the competition. They are stuck in the "survival stage" of adaptation and sometimes do little more than make ends meet.

Successful organizations recognize that adaptation is only one part of the success formula. The catalyst for success is innovation.

A great way to understand innovation is to view it as an ecosystem.

> In the 1930s, British botanist Arthur Tansley introduced the term 'ecosystem' to describe a community of organisms interacting with each other and their environments — air, water, earth, etc. In order to *thrive*, these organisms compete and collaborate with each other on available resources, co-evolve, and jointly adapt to external disruptions. [xxxiv]

Businesses also "compete and collaborate with each other on available resources, co-evolve, and jointly adapt to external disruptions." How the business adapts and innovates determines its success or failure.

> A business ecosystem is the network of organizations — including suppliers, distributors, customers, competitors, government agencies, and so on — involved in the delivery of a specific product or service through both competition and cooperation. The idea is that each entity in the ecosystem affects and is affected by the others, creating a constantly evolving relationship in which each entity must be flexible and adaptable in order to survive, as in a biological ecosystem. [xxxv]

Innovation requires adaptation or evolution, understanding of the environment, competition, cooperation, and making the most effective use of all available resources – just like ecosystems.

Just as adaptation is a key to survival, innovation is the key to thriving. All businesses, all people, all systems want to do more than survive and struggle. All success-minded businesses, people, and systems want to thrive.

> My mission in life is not merely to survive, but to thrive; and to do so with some passion, some compassion, some humor, and some style. – Maya Angelou

Innovation transcends the axiom of "adapt or die." Innovation pushes, and compels, and opens doors, and motivates, and is the engine of success.

Wikipedia.org defines innovation as:

> ...the implementation of a new or significantly improved idea, good, service, process or practice that is intended to be useful. Scholars who have studied innovation generally differentiate among five main types of innovation:
>
> 1. <u>Product innovation</u>, which involves the introduction of a new good or service that is substantially improved. This might include improvements in functional characteristics, technical abilities, ease of use, or any other dimension.
> 2. <u>Process innovation</u>, involves the implementation of a new or significantly improved production or delivery method.
> 3. <u>Marketing innovation,</u> is the development of new marketing methods with improvement in product design or packaging, product promotion or pricing.
> 4. <u>Organizational innovation</u>, (also referred as social innovation) involves the creation of new organizations, business practices, ways of running organizations or new organizational behavior.
> 5. <u>Business Model innovation</u>, involves changing the way business is done in terms of capturing value. [xxxvi]

Successful businesses have leaders who are deliberate, skillful, and agile enough to maneuver through these five innovation types.

In the business world, the late Steve Jobs and innovation were synonymous. His founding and management roles in Apple, NeXT, and Pixar demonstrated a mastery of the five innovation types. During his stewardship of Apple, he shepherded the Macintosh computer through its evolution, revitalized the digital music industry with iTunes and the iPod, transformed the mobile phone industry with the iPhone, revolutionized portable computing with the iPad, and modernized access to digital content with Apple TV. Even after his death, the companies and products Steve Jobs touched continue to innovate.

In nature, the Galápagos Islands demonstrate innovation with one of the most unique ecosystems in the world.

> There are more than 500 plant species found on the Galapagos, about one-third of which are endemic, meaning they're native to the islands and found nowhere else in the world. Exclusive species of cotton, guava, passion flower, pepper and tomatoes all grow here.
>
> ...The Galápagos Islands are important because of these endemic species -- there are roughly 9,000 species living on the islands and in surrounding waters. Fourteen distinct subspecies of giant tortoise live

on the islands… as well as the only tropical-dwelling penguins. There are several reptile species including land and marine iguanas (marine iguanas are the only lizard known to swim in the ocean), lava lizards, geckos and snakes, 1,600 species of insects and 400 species of fish.[xxxvii]

The flora and fauna innovate and thrive by adapting to the changes in their environment and using those changes to their advantage.

Apple and the Galápagos Islands are similar because they thrive in the changing conditions of their respective environments. They thrive because they pay attention to their surroundings, adapt when changes occur, and take risks.

If you do not try anything, "…new or significantly improved [whether it is an] idea, a good, a service, a process or a practice that is intended to be useful…"[xxxviii] then you cannot expect to thrive.

Innovation inherently involves risk, which is a necessary part of growth in nature and in business. We do not know all the species that did not survive the changes of time and environment on the Galápagos Islands, and we may never know all the failed attempts at product creation that Steve Jobs endured, but we do know that there were mistakes and setbacks. We also know that no matter the setbacks or changes they kept innovating.

Companies that have a desire to be the best must have more than a survivor's mentality; they must resolve to thrive. They must take risks, have a vision, a plan for success, and the ability to execute the plan. They must be committed to innovation.

How we apply these ideals to our individual actions and our corporate practices determines just how successful we can be.

Adapt and Survive – Innovate and Thrive

Integrity is the lifeblood of democracy. Deceit is a poison in its veins. – Edward Kennedy

Integrity: The Foundation Of Leadership, Individual, And Organizational Success

To be successful in business, leaders need to provide a service or product that people want, deliver excellent customer service, and be innovative in how they think, act, and create. These ideas are important to business success, but integrity is crucial for self-worth, moral surety, and excellence in leadership.

In 2006 I read an article by Chris Zach Hidalgo, titled, The Definition of Integrity. In the article, Chris defines integrity as a skill, a learned behavior that can be mastered over a lifetime of practice. He views integrity as an application of appropriate behavior in all aspects of personal and professional life.

I was impressed by the completeness of his understanding of the essence of integrity and am honored to share the article in its entirety with the permission of the author.

Definition of Integrity
==

By: Chris Zach Hidalgo
Monday December 16, 2002
webweevers.com/integrity.htm
==
According to Merriam Webster, integrity is:
1: firm adherence to a code of especially moral or artistic values: **INCORRUPTIBILITY**
2: an unimpaired condition: **SOUNDNESS**
3: the quality or state of being complete or undivided: **COMPLETENESS**
synonym see **HONESTY**

The following information is simply an opinion based on life experiences and a personal understanding of truth and honesty--which are part of the foundational aspects of true integrity.

Integrity is A Skill
Integrity is similar to a skill. A qualified carpenter must endure years of training, practice and exposure to building materials and circumstances that call for his talent. Integrity must also endure years of practice and exposure for integrity is NOT necessarily inherent within a person's personality. Instead, integrity is a trait that is taught and learned over an entire lifetime--as long as you're alive, anyway.

Point of reference
Integrity is a guideline, a benchmark, a point of reference or a goal that is used to make decisions that rely on truth and honesty. All things are related to this point of reference and judged accordingly. To maintain integrity, you

must remember to refer to truth and honesty in ALL decisions, thoughts and actions. That's not an option if you are to have integrity.

A great tower
Integrity is something that a person builds and maintains during a lifetime. You can consider integrity as a building within a person's heart that starts when the person is young. This "building" begins with the first hole that is dug. Once the hole is dug, the foundation is laid--usually by parents and other leaders (church and school instructors). The walls follow with windows and doors added along the way. The windows would allow for transparency and serve as a type of checks-and-balances. The doors would allow for modifications of a person's definition of integrity to easily take place--hopefully for the better. The roof is added later and serves to protect from outside forces.

Rebuilding
Just as you can rebuild a house when it falls down, so too can you reestablish integrity if you fall away from its blessings.

A plant
Integrity can also be considered as a seed. It is planted in youth, watered in childhood and blossoms in adulthood. The more you water it throughout life, the more it grows and blooms. Just as it is with plants, if neglected at any point, it WILL wither and die. If your plant has died, simply plant a new seed and water it daily! Note that a plant does not blossom immediately but must go through a life cycle first. So, integrity will take a while to get used to...again.

Maintenance
Integrity must be maintained. A janitor cleans and straightens rooms for a living. You must be a janitor and maintain true integrity. If you avoid the dust that settles, your definition of integrity begins to diminish and decrease in value. A strict maintenance schedule must be kept or what has taken a lifetime to build will come crumbling down in minutes.

Loss
It's critical to note that integrity can be lost or compromised beyond recognition in a person's life. I've been there and am in the process of reestablishing integrity in my life...and it's not easy. Recognizing that integrity has been compromised or is totally lost from your life is the first step of many. The second step is to do something about it--and that would be to make the decision to plant a new seed and water it daily...even minute-to-minute.

Holding up to the test
Consider a cup that cannot hold water. A person that lives their life without integrity is like that cup. The crack may be invisible to the eye, but if it doesn't hold up to the test, it's virtually worthless. Many people walk around with a small crack that is easily hidden, but time reveals their flaw.

Other definitions
People can tweak or modify their definition of integrity to suit their needs, desires and ambitions at the time. For that reason, it's possible to have a large number of definitions of the word or state of affairs in a person's life--but that doesn't necessarily mean they're all sound definitions.

Integrity WILL:

- Begin and continue as a personal ON-GOING decision to stand firm on principals that are inherently good.
- Most likely take the long, straight and narrow road and does not cave into cheating.
- Tell the truth over a lie despite the consequences.
- Suffer the consequences instead of compromise itself.
- Help to steer a person clear of those that easily bow to a corrupt nature.
- Be apt to lend a helping hand simply as a by-product of this special lifestyle decision.
- Diminish and eventually disappear if you choose to ignore and abandon its blessing.
- Set you apart from a great number of people who have chosen to follow the lead of a different drummer.
- Sometimes separate you from the "in" crowd, but that's not always the case.
- On some occasions, make other people feel uncomfortable around you because of their own insecurities, problems and guilt.
- Impress others only because of your decision to adhere to such a (sometimes) difficult lifestyle.
- Sometimes put you into tight situations that APPEAR to be needlessly difficult.
- Allow for rebuilding. It will come back and continue to blossom if you choose and allow it to grow within.

Integrity will NOT:

- Allow for decisions that may compromise personal belief and faith.
- Always APPEAR to help a situation.

- Be an easy decision for all situations.
- Be Disneyland and roses all the time.
- Give in to peer pressure simply because "everyone's doing it."
- Give up on you--you can always reestablish integrity by making a conscious effort to rebuild what past mistakes have broken down.
- In an obvious way come to the rescue of a person.

Benefits
Integrity always benefits a person, but the benefit is NOT always immediately recognizable. In fact, sometimes the benefits of Integrity are not obvious for many years down the road. It's possible for a person to live most of their lives and not see the benefits of integrity until late in life. It's different for everyone and doesn't mean it's better or worse for you, it just means it's different, that's all.

Notice
As a side note, please know that in many cases, "things are not as they appear."

Experiences
Integrity is NOT a one-time experience or situation. Instead, Integrity is an on-going experience of situations where sound decisions are made based on good judgment, wisdom and knowledge.

By-Products
Integrity has its by-products. As you become more familiar with a lifestyle that allows for integrity to bloom wild and free, life is usually filled with more and more peace--a by-product. After a while of on-going decisions guided by integrity, people begin to take notice. Employers begin to place more trust in you and your abilities. Friends rely more and more on your apparent wisdom. Better decisions lead to a better life.

Misdirected hate
As a direct result of your decision to establish integrity within yourself, you will gain favor with many people. Others will hate you for it--another by-product. People hate other people for the weirdest reasons. Someone dedicated to truth and honesty is a typical target. There are many reasons for this misdirected hate, but the most common reason is their own insecurity (referring to the person who hates). People WILL be threatened by you because of your decision to maintain integrity.

Personal definition
This personal definition of integrity is an attempt to offer an unbiased

presentation of what integrity can and cannot mean. That is to say this definition of integrity:

- Is in no way the one-and-only true definition.
- May actually serve to corrupt someone's definition of integrity--BUT this definition has a sincere intention to help explain the many sides of integrity's purity and benefits so that the reader can decide for themselves.
- Should help to answer some of the many questions people may have about integrity and the possible role it may play in a person's life, decision making, thoughts, actions and destiny.
- Should broaden one's insight about how much of a role integrity plays in their daily life, even minute-to-minute.

The great cathedral
Remember, you can live life the way you want, for good or for evil. But I'd like to suggest the following story for your consideration:

Back in the Middle Ages (1200–1600 A.D.) a great cathedral was being built by many skilled laborers. One day a strange man came to town and asked each of the men what they were doing. One man answered, "I have to lay this brick to feed my nagging wife and my many ungrateful children." Another answered by saying, "I'm just trying to pass the time until I die and at the same time keep myself afloat." Another man said, "I'm following my father's footsteps and doing what I'm told." An old man answered, "I am a mason, this is what I do." Yet another man was heard saying, "I do this because I have many debts to pay."

Then the stranger saw a young man laying brick who was working feverishly unlike the other workers. Intrigued, the stranger questioned this young man next. After being questioned, the young man stopped, starred at the yet unfinished building and answered by saying, "I am taking part in the greatest building project in history. A cathedral unlike any other in the world. One of surpassing beauty and size. This cathedral will be the greatest the world has ever seen. I'm only laying the block, but my efforts will help this great cathedral to stand the test of time so future generations can marvel at and appreciate its awesome beauty."

Needless to say, it's not what you have to do, what you want to do or what you think you should do, but how you do all things.

How you do what you have to do, what you want to do and what you think you should do will determine your success. You will have to do things, want to do things and think you should do things your whole life, but it's the quality of how you do them that really matters.

Integrity plays a critical part in quality decisions, thoughts and actions. It will be obvious in how you act and react to expected and unexpected circumstances.

A wonderful life
Choosing a wonderful life over (just) life can make the difference between success and failure, peace and chaos, love and hate, and integrity plays a key role in those decisions.

Chose to be like the young man laying the brick to build what he believes to be the greatest cathedral in the whole world.
Chose to plant a seed that will become the immovable oak.
Chose to be like the janitor that maintains a clean household.
Chose to be a cup that can hold water and is half full instead of half empty.
You can do it, it's as simple as a decision--one of many that will be based on wisdom, good judgment and knowledge.

Chose to incorporate integrity in your life today.

That is integrity.

Defining Integrity In A Nutshell

...or in this case, in a fortune cookie.

The other day I was having lunch with two friends at a Chinese restaurant in Flagstaff, Arizona when I received an interesting "fortune" from the traditional after-dinner fortune cookie (that I usually smash on the table, work through the pieces for the "fortune," then consider the alleged "fortune" and toss what's left--I don't like the cookie, just the fortune):

On this particular day the unusually unique "fortune" read:

Integrity is doing the right thing, even if nobody is watching.

After I stopped coughing and finally got some air as a result of the shock of reading something so prevalent in my constant search to define words that I want to apply to my life, I realized that this "fortune" was by far the most profound, applicable and true "fortune" cookie I had ever received.

Such a simple yet concise definition of the word integrity from a fortune cookie? I could hardly believe it!

All text on this page is copyrighted © 2002+ - All rights reserved.

NOTICE: I trust you will not take credit for my writing and will practice the integrity the material speaks about in your desire to quote my work.[xxxix]

CHAPTER TWO

LEADERSHIP COMMUNICATION

Words are singularly the most powerful force available to humanity. We can choose to use this force constructively with words of encouragement, or destructively using words of despair. Words have energy and power with the ability to help, to heal, to hinder, to hurt, to harm, to humiliate and to humble. — Yehuda Berg

LEADERSHIP COMMUNICATION

Effective Communication

What is communication?

Merriam Webster defines communication as, "the act or process of using words, sounds, signs, or behaviors to express or exchange information or to express your ideas, thoughts, feelings, etc., to someone else."[xl]

Communication is not only about the words we use, it is also about the images, icons, and standards we display to convey a message. Our body language, the way we dress, the way we stand, smile, smirk, use our hands, etc., communicates *something* to others, whether that is what we intended to communicate or not.

Everything we do to communicate can be muddled through the prism and perception of our audience. The words we use, the way we speak, the tone, style, rhythm, emphasis, setting, and passion in which we communicate determines if we can connect with others to develop understanding.

Leaders must recognize that adhering to a simple definition of communication is not always useful. We need to work toward <u>effective communication</u>, defined as:

> The act of expressing or exchanging information, ideas, thoughts, feelings, etc., to someone else, and having the information received and understood in the way that was intended.

At times, the way we communicate has a negative or hurtful impact on others. If this was not the intent, it can lead to awkward moments at best and ruined reputations and relationships at worst. One of the most formidable challenges in communication effectiveness is recognizing the difference between communication <u>intent</u> and communication <u>impact</u>.

Effective leaders practice and hone their communication skills. They not only focus on information sharing, but on developing context and connection, checking for understanding not just acknowledgment, and are agile enough to move through the "minefield-of-myriad-multimodal-communication" including, understanding the setting, community, cultural, environmental, social or affinity group, etc., to connect with their audience.

The *minefield-of-myriad-multimodal-communication*, refers to the reality that at any given moment in the communication process information sharing must pass through the perception, mood, understanding, biases, etc., of the speaker and the hearer and can change at any moment based on those same criteria.

This is not easy stuff. Remember, communication is a critical component of SCD. We need to develop *effective* communication skills to truly connect with others. This is especially true for leaders trying to create dynamic and engaged organizations.

In his book <u>Leadership A to Z</u>, James O'toole states:

> The task of a leader is to communicate clearly and repeatedly the organization's vision, strategy, goals and objectives, and to communicate its values, missions, purpose, and principles - all with the intent of helping every person involved understand what work needs to be done and why, and what part each individual plays in the overall effort.[xli]

Many organizations make their mission and goals public, they hang them on plaques, post them in newsletters, place them on business cards, etc. But how should leaders act to make the mission and goals more than just words?

Bill Gore, the founder of W. L. Gore and Associates, the makers of Gore-Tex®, told employees to "go find something useful to do." He did not want anyone to be limited by a position, a title, or a hierarchy while trying to enhance the success of the business. He knew that the organization was run by competent, capable, innovative people who could rise to challenges and overcome obstacles if they were encouraged and empowered to do so.

Leaders should encourage <u>all</u> staff to think about the larger success of the organization. Do not restrict your teams to thinking only about their specific departments or their individual tasks. If team members complete their work and meet the departmental goals, let them lend their skills and creativity to the entire organization.

The actions of all employees, *collectively*, determines if a company succeeds. Leaders should acknowledge and reward positive behavior, and address and correct negative behavior. They should provide appropriate and constructive feedback, lend a helping hand, and hold themselves accountable to do their best. The role leaders play in directing, encouraging, and engaging their teams is essential to organizational success.

Communicating ideas effectively is an essential part of leadership. Listening effectively is an essential part of communication. All organizations should demonstrate their commitment to listening to and acting on the ideas of their employees. Encourage and empower your employees and see just how successful your organization can be.

What skills are necessary to communicate effectively?

- Clarity of thought in spoken and written form
- The ability to engage with others
- Appropriateness
- Understanding your audience
- Knowledge of the topic or material
- Trustworthiness

Communication is a minefield filled with uncertainty and risk. A common phrase, joke, or expression used in or with one community, social group, or affinity group can have dire consequences when used with another.

Our words matter. Leaders must build trust, engage with their audience and create a connection so that even when the words used are imprecise or imperfect, they receive the benefit-of-the-doubt that the intent was honorable.

We mitigate the risk of having communication errors when we learn about others, discover our own biases and blind spots, pay attention to reactions and responses to our words, apologize when we misspeak, and learn how to truly listen to others.

One of the best tools to support listening skills, develop understanding, and connect with individuals and teams is called the TDC Communication Exercise. It is a simple and effective way to establish positive intent, understanding, and engagement one-on-one and in group settings.

The TDC Communication Exercise consists of four questions:

> 1. **How do you communicate with others?**
>
> 2. **How do you want others to communicate with you?**
>
> 3. **What are your hot buttons?**
>
> 4. **How will we communicate with each other as a group (or in a group setting)?**

Question four (4) focuses on team dynamics as opposed to individual needs. The team collectively and collaboratively creates standards for engagement and reaches consensus on the communication expectations.

This exercise provides an opportunity for individuals to share their communication expectations and name their hot buttons – things that erode trust. This is crucial for understanding the best methods to connect with others. Miscommunication – literally not being able to share a message in a way that an individual can hear, digest, and act on – is a significant roadblock to effective communication.

Hot Buttons

"Hot Buttons" are statements and actions that illicit a strong negative emotional response from the person receiving the information. They are typically connected to words or behaviors that cause a visceral or instinctively raw response and trigger a fight-or-flight impulse.

Hot buttons are connected to actions that cause emotional pain, embarrassment, and perceived disrespect. Pressing an individual's hot buttons undermines trust and blocks effective communication. Hot button issues often pose a dilemma, as individuals protect themselves from feeling vulnerable by not sharing with others the very behaviors that make them feel vulnerable.

Unfortunately, when we do not share our hot buttons with others, especially friends, family, colleagues, and supervisors (those who are more constant in our lives), they may push them out of ignorance. We then decide to label their actions as intentional while they *may* simply be communication errors.

When our hot buttons are pushed repeatedly by the same people, we often develop defensive or survival responses that create additional barriers to engagement.

Revealing our emotional triggers is a leap of faith but doing so can allow for discovery of an individual's "true intent." If we do not share our communication needs, we cannot expect others to truly understand how their behaviors impact us.

By not sharing our hot buttons we miss an opportunity to strengthen relationships.

Asking people to share their hot button issues – their vulnerabilities – can be intimidating, but it can reap significant rewards. By listening, we can avoid communication landmines that undermine relationships, e.g., inappropriate jokes, perceived condescending statements, patronizing behaviors, trigger words, etc.

When leaders listen, choose to communicate effectively, and behave in a manner that respects the communication needs of others, trust is developed.

NOTE: When individuals share their communication styles and hot buttons, the information should be treated as a gift. Recognize that participants have made themselves vulnerable in an attempt to enhance or develop trust. Do not undermine that trust by misusing the information.

The TDC Communication Exercise

All individuals have choices. We have the choice to share our needs, wants, and concerns with others, or keep them hidden. We have the choice to listen and engage with others as they would like to be engaged. If we want to understand those around us, we must first learn how to effectively communicate on a 1:1 basis. The most effective way to understand an individual's communication needs is to ask, and then listen to the response.

The TDC Communication Exercise provides an opportunity to honestly address the communication desires and needs of individuals and groups.

In this exercise, individuals write down their communication styles, needs, and concerns and share them with the group. The participants then come to consensus on their group communication needs. Enough time should be allotted to allow participants to answer the questions and discuss the feelings and thoughts generated by each answer.

Questions for individuals:

1. **How do you communicate with others?**
2. **How do you want others to communicate with you?**
3. **What are your hot buttons?**

The group will then come to consensus on the communication expectations for the team.

Question for the group/team:

4. **How will we communicate with each other as a group, or in a group setting?**

Outline:

- To start the exercise, allocate 5 minutes for individuals to write down their responses to questions 1–3. (Note: *The questions can also be provided in advance, to give participants more time to think through their responses.*)
- Participants should be informed that their answers will be collected and distributed to facilitate ongoing communication with the entire team.
- After all participants have finished writing their answers, they should discuss them with the entire group. Individuals should be allowed enough time to present their answers without interruption. This is primarily a listening exercise. Questions can be asked, but they should be directed to the individual after they have answered all three questions.

The team will then discuss question number 4. Answers should be written for all participants to see. The team should come to consensus on how they will communicate as a team in meetings and group settings.

After each participant has shared their communication styles, their answers should be collected and consolidated for distribution to all members of the team.

Discussion: Up to this point, you may not have had prior experience or knowledge of other members' communication needs. Therefore, communication mistakes may have occurred. If possible, forgive the mistakes. You now have relevant information on the communication needs of your team members. The choice is yours to support or disregard their communication needs.

It is imperative that you do not make light of, tease, joke, or use the information gathered about individuals' hot buttons as a weapon. You will undermine trust and sabotage your relationship.

Listed below are sample responses to the TDC Communication Exercise.

COMMUNICATION EXPECTATIONS ANSWERS

How Do I Communicate With Others?

- If you ask, I will give my opinion.
- I will share criticism with you in private.
- I am very aware of my non-verbal expressions and use them to make my point.
- Regarding work, I am direct, to the point, sometimes curt.
- If it is a personal matter, I am not always direct.

How Do I Want Others To Communicate With Me?

- Give feedback even if I do not ask (with caution).
- Do not whine.
- Give me details.
- Be prepared.

Hot Buttons

- People who do not respect others' things.
- Sexual comments in the workplace.
- Know-it-alls.
- Habitual tardiness, laziness, forgetfulness.
- I do not like being put on the spot.

Communication As A Staff Team

- Stick with the schedule/be timely.
- Be respectful of the speaker.
- Give constructive criticism.
- Come organized with what you want to accomplish.
- Put it in writing.
- Be focused on the moment.

Communication Exercise Worksheet

1. How do you communicate with others?

2. How do you want others to communicate with you?

3. What are your hot buttons?

4. How will we communicate with each other as a group, or in a group setting?

In true dialogue, both sides are willing to change. —
Nhat Hanh

Dialogue, A Key To Understanding

I have been a consultant on issues of effective communication with an emphasis on race since 1992. I co-founded The Dialogue Consultants with friends and colleagues after the 1992 civil unrest in Los Angeles following the acquittal of the officers in the Rodney King beating. We worked with many communities on the difficult issues of race, oppression, privilege, and identity development, and were dedicated to helping individuals and communities understand themselves, learn to understand others, and foster cooperation and healing through facilitated dialogue.

The need for dialogue is just as important today. The numerous videos showing officer-involved shootings of African Americans and a resurgence in anti-Semitic demonstrations has caused a new sense of outrage and urgency. I am encouraged by the leadership demonstrated in many communities to bridge the divides and work for positive change, but I am also saddened by the lines drawn in the sand by others.

Similar to the aftermath of the civil unrest in 1992, people are "talking" about strengthening relations between communities of difference but are unable to effectively discuss the difficult issues of racism and inequality.

Language is important. How we phrase our thoughts and feelings is important, how we express ourselves and whether we believe we are heard is important. It is difficult to engage with others across racial lines or any lines of difference if we are trying to be perfect in our communication. Unfortunately, because of this unrealistic desire, many people abandon the opportunity to come together and end up holding on to their beliefs and assumptions about the "other."

How do we hold meaningful conversations when we do not know how to talk with one another? Just as important, how do we begin meaningful conversations when we do not know how to listen to one another?

When we are entrenched in our own beliefs, we are unable to speak so that others can hear the full meaning of our words or listen for understanding and common ground. We are invested in winning an argument as opposed to understanding the other person.

As I listen to the conversations around these current racially charged events, it is apparent that we do not know how to understand each other. One group wants intellectually "safe" conversations, devoid of emotion, while others want conversations full of passion, energy, and an acceptance of their experience. Both groups demand that the only way to have *real, honest* conversations is to conform to their preferred method of communication.

I would suggest a compromise and offer tools that promote understanding.

Reaching understanding requires that individuals:

- Stop being incontrovertibly entrenched in their own beliefs.
- Engage in dialogue not debate.
- Develop skills to facilitate effective communication.
- Choose to care.

1. – <u>Being entrenched</u> in our beliefs blocks us from making real connections with others. Entrenchment keeps us from being able to hear any ideas, statements, or facts that do not conform to what we already believe. Disrupting entrenchment requires us to be open to the possibility that we may not have all the answers.

2. – <u>Dialogue</u> is a radically different way of communicating than many of us are accustomed to.

…Dialogue moves beyond any one individual's understanding to build collective understanding and meaning. It helps make explicit the implicit and can build and sustain community. In dialogue, we do not try to convince others of our point of view. There is no emphasis on winning but rather on collaboration and synthesis of points of view. Developing a collective meaning or understanding is the objective of dialogue. – Edgar H. Schein

3. – <u>Facilitation</u> means making something easier. The facilitation of a dialogue session involves assisting or guiding people in the process of change, so that they achieve desired goals or outcomes in a caring and considerate manner. A facilitator creates and maintains an environment that enables another person or group to do its work.

4. – <u>Choosing to care</u> or demonstrating the value of caring, involves being present in the moment through all the stress, pain, and emotional turmoil of the

conversation and maintaining your dignity and the dignity of the person/people you are with. Demonstrating the value of caring requires that we remain open and aware of our fears, anxiety, stereotypes, and emotions and stay in the conversation without panic. It requires that we care for the other person – not in the abstract - but in a deeply personal and committed manner. It requires us to be honest and vulnerable, a position many of us avoid.

Nowhere in these four concepts is there an expectation that a person change their beliefs, values, or be disingenuous. These ideas require a sincere desire to understand differences without making assumptions about an individual's motivation. There is no requirement to adopt another person's perspective, but if we can understand why people believe what they do or understand how they came to their conclusions, we can make more informed decisions on how we interact. Respecting each other's experience and hearing each other's story is critical to understanding motivation.

These ideas require that we work toward understanding, which necessitates a level of empathy far greater than what is demonstrated in many of the conversations taking place now. What we currently have is an "I'm right, you're wrong" mentality, which leads to more entrenched beliefs.

To work through these feelings effectively we must ask the question, "What if what the other person is telling me is true for them?" We must *choose* to not instantly dismiss statements or ideas we disagree with. This requires that we *choose* not to be ruled by our fears, learned responses, history, stereotypes, or socialized behaviors.

These are difficult concepts to overcome because we must *unlearn* so much misinformation about the "other."

To be clear, there is no expectation to put yourself at risk in an attempt to understand another person's hate, biases, or prejudices. There may be no way to effectively dialogue with someone rooted in a philosophy of hate, supremacy, or violence against those different from themselves or their identity groups.

Can we truly dialogue? Can we set our assumptions aside, our political affiliations, our religious and cultural norms, and our deeply held beliefs about the other? If we lowered our walls to truly dialogue…what would happen?

The Dialogue Consultants created the Tools for Dialogue and the Nine (9) Skills for Facilitation© to support productive and impactful dialogue on issues of race. But these tools can be used to support engaged conversations on any number of difficult issues.

Before you review the tools, answer the following questions:

- Are you willing to be wrong?
- Are you willing to endure the pain of misunderstanding and mistakes, but continue to press forward?
- Are you willing to be vulnerable?
- Are you willing to stop investing in your assumptions about others' motivations?
- Are you willing to listen for understanding and not just to the imperfect words someone uses?
- Are you willing to explore your own imperfections?
- Do you care enough to look at the imperfections of others and still see them as valuable human beings?

Leaders must gain an understanding of the power of effective dialogue and hone their facilitation skills to engage with groups, teams, and the organizations they serve.

The Role Of Dialogue

What is Dialogue?

One might think of dialogue as a stream of meaning flowing among and through a group of people, out of which might emerge some new understanding, something creative. Dialogue moves beyond any one individual's understanding to build collective understanding and meaning. It helps make explicit the implicit and can build and sustain community. In dialogue, we do not try to convince others of our point of view. There is no emphasis on winning but rather on collaboration and synthesis of points of view. Developing a collective meaning or understanding is the objective of dialogue. – Edgar H. Schein

Tools for Dialogue[xlii]

- Acknowledge another's feelings.
- Understand the difference between releasing emotion and information sharing.
- Ask a clarifying question that deepens your understanding of another's opinion: "Can you help me understand…"
- Make your assumptions known to others: "Here is what I think and how I got there…"
- Talk about your feelings/emotions without blaming.
- Talk about your needs without demanding.
- State your opinions even if they are not fully developed.
- Find the truth in what you oppose and the error in what you espouse.
- Listen without judging and without making interruptions – stop your internal dialogue.
- If you get defensive, recognize it, acknowledge it, take a breath, and ask for support.
- Ask questions about others' assumptions and data without evoking defensiveness: "I would like to understand that better…"
- If you are stating a fact, provide "observable data" to back up what you have said.
- If your "buttons" are pushed, try to surface the scenarios in your mind that pushed your buttons.

Why Dialogue?

Preparing to Dialogue:

> That we desperately need more open talk on this issue -- both within individual communities and between different communities -- is beyond question. Whether we have the courage, patience and sensitivity to conduct such highly charged dialogues at this time remains to be seen. - Richard Yarborough

- Dialogue is collaborative: two or more sides work together toward a common understanding.
- Dialogue assumes that many people have pieces of the answer and that together they can put them into a workable solution.
- Dialogue reveals assumptions for reevaluation.
- Dialogue causes introspection on one's own position.
- Dialogue enlarges and possibly changes a participant's point of view.
- Dialogue creates an open-minded attitude: an openness to being wrong and openness to change.
- In dialogue one listens to understand the other side, find meaning and basic agreement.
- In dialogue one searches for strength in other positions.
- Dialogue involves real concern for the other person and seeks not to alienate or defend.[xliii]

> We live in a society where we define politeness in a way that encourages avoidance. So, it is impolite to confront a reality that may be unpleasant for a moment, even if we realize that it might bring us to a better situation ultimately. – Jackie Dupont Walkers

Nine (9) Essential Skills For Facilitation

Facilitators help create and maintain an environment that enables individuals and groups to work collaboratively. These nine skills provide a foundation for engagement that is effective and practical for all leaders.

Nine (9) Skills for Facilitation©

  (a) Description of the skill.
  (b) Context for use.
  (c) Example(s) of the skills.

1. Validate someone's experience

a) The skill is to let someone know they have been heard and to help them feel that they are "okay."
b) This is needed if someone has taken a risk and the group may not validate the person. At times, you may need to validate someone before you challenge them. The response should be sincere. Try to find something about what the person said that is true, helpful, or commendable.
c) "Thanks for bringing that perspective in." "It took a lot to be honest like that." "Thank you for helping us see this issue from another point of view." "It really makes sense that you were feeling X."

2. Listen without judgment – bracketing judgments

a) The skill is to allow all ideas and feelings to come to your mind but set them in [brackets] for a period of time so that you can remain present in the moment. It is *difficult* not to form opinions, but you do not have to act on them the moment they occur. At the same time, you may need to consciously say to yourself something like, "I know I do not agree, but I need to listen to hear this person's opinion."
b) This is needed when someone says something you disagree with or says something in a manner you have a reaction to. This is helpful because we often "turn off" when someone uses words, a style, or a cliché, that pushes our buttons.
c) *This skill is an internal process, not something stated out loud.*

3. Synthesize information

a) The skill is to objectively state what you have heard without adding your own assumptions.
b) This is needed to allow the conversation to "land" somewhere for a minute. This allows participants to decide where they want to go next. This is especially helpful, if the dialogue has been on one topic for a long time, if the dialogue does not seem to be meeting the group's goals, or if people seem to be talking past one another.
c) "What I have been hearing is…" "Let me try to summarize what I have heard, and you should let me know if I am off the mark."

4. Help someone rephrase a question/statement for clarity and understanding

a) The skill is to avoid judging someone while guiding them to ask the question in another form.
b) Rephrasing can be helpful if someone has not *really* asked a question, if they have been telling a personal story, asked too long of a question, or if they have asked a trick question.
c) "What is at the heart of your question?" "We can go in a lot of directions with that question. Is there one main question you would like to start with?" or "Is there another way to ask that question that does not really assume an answer?"

5. Ask questions without bringing in judgments

a) The skill is to ask for clarification, ask for more information, or ask the group what they want to do next, without making a judgment about what was just said. For example, if you feel impatient about what someone is saying, you need to find a way to be honest but not judgmental about your impatience, or not bring that impatience into your question.
b) This is needed whenever you are asking a question of an individual or the group.
c) "I want to find out where you are going with the question. Could you take a step back, and talk about what is behind the question?"

6. Identify and challenge assumptions

a) The skill is to hear what someone has said, but to help them unearth the often-hidden assumptions that lie beneath the statement or question. You should not assume you know what the assumption is.
b) This is needed when someone accidentally or purposefully hides an

assumption within a question or statement. Often, our statements are built on a "ladder of assumptions," and once we climb down that ladder we find more common meaning and understanding.
c) "When you said that, I heard another question being asked, behind that question. Was there an assumption behind your question?" "Your answer seems to be built on some prior experience or information. Could you tell the group a little more about how you came up with that belief?"

7. Challenge a statement without de-valuing the person

a) The skill is to first validate and say what you heard that is true or meaningful to you and then provide another perspective. In most cases, your perspective should be offered as an opinion. Because you have more power in the group, people will take an authoritative statement as "The Truth" and potentially an end of the conversation.
b) This is needed if someone states opinion as fact or if someone is bringing in false or stereotypical information. It may be needed if someone is infringing on the ground rules set by the group.
c) "Thank you for bringing that perspective in. I would like to provide an alternative way of looking at it. Feel free to ask a follow-up question if it does not fit with your ideas." "Could you say more about that idea? I am wondering what you are basing your ideas on and if you could provide some examples or evidence?"

8. Provide information/teach while maintaining collegiality (peership)

a) The skill is to provide information in as brief a format as possible, to state it in a way that invites a response, as opposed to ends the conversation, and that does not discount anyone's feelings.
b) If someone has stated an opinion as fact; if someone has presented stereotypical or false information.
c) "I can see how you could draw that conclusion from your experience. I would like to present another way of looking at that." "From my reading and experience, I have found different information…"

9. Recognize the teachable moments

a) Paying attention to those moments when a simple statement or action provides an opening or insight that helps someone grow or helps the group take a step forward.
b) When you recognize a shift in conversation, an "ah hah" moment, or a perceived opening to learning something new, or acceptance of a different

point of view.
c) "What you said is very important. Can you talk about what spurred that thought/feeling?" "It seems as if you have made a breakthrough. How do you feel about what you just said?" "We just learned something important" or "What was shared was very important, do you understand the impact of the statement?"

There are many skills necessary to serve as an effective leader and facilitator, but a mastery of the Tools For Dialogue and the Nine (9) Skills for Facilitation© can enhance your ability to engage in dialogue not debate, communicate effectively through difficult issues, and assist individuals and teams in reaching their goals.

Behavior is the mirror in which everyone shows their image. — Johann Wolfgang von Goethe

Behavior in leadership: "Behavior Breeds Behavior"

The most accomplished communicator can undermine their message if they behave in a manner incongruent with their speech.

I was asked to teach a leadership course using a training video called, <u>If Looks Could Kill, The Power Of Behaviour</u>. The focus of the video was on customer service and how an individual's "behaviors" or actions can "breed" positive or negative behaviors in others and influence the customer experience. The original 1986 video was in the form of a murder mystery produced by Video Arts, a UK company associated with John Cleese of Monty Python fame.

The central theme of the video is that behavior is a choice. How we respond to a given situation is in our control, and <u>our</u> actions can cause positive or negative reactions in others.

Our emotions, how we feel in each moment when our buttons are pushed, may be spontaneous, but our response – our behavior – is something that we must own and manage. We always have choices; how we choose to act can support or undermine our business and personal relationships, our reputation, and ultimately determine our character.

Although <u>If Looks Could Kill, The Power of Behaviour</u> was created primarily to help front-line employees learn how their behaviors can impact customers' attitudes and actions, the information is helpful for all interpersonal encounters and includes practical tips on how best to greet clients, the importance of being present, and the necessity of being appropriate.

The concepts of "Behavior Breeds Behavior" are simple:

- Greet your colleagues and clients with respect.
- Maintain and practice patience, understanding, and professionalism.
- Be appropriate with humor.

There are 5-core principles associated with behavior in the video:

1. The way people behave toward you is usually dictated by the way you behave toward them.

2. Observe the behavior and the response [and reflect on how your behaviors may have influenced the interaction.]

3. You choose your behavior:
   - Behavior is not something you are born with; it is a choice. You choose your behavior whenever you interact with the public.

4. You can use your behavior to help or hinder a transaction:
   - Verbally
     - Acknowledge people as soon as possible.
     - Apologize for any delay.
     - Use a person's name (when it is given).
     - Confirm that you are listening.
     - Check that you have understood, agree upon the next steps, and provide options whenever possible.
   - Visually
     - Be friendly and welcoming.
     - Look at people with an attentive look or gesture.
     - Lean forward and use open gestures.

5. Behavior can be used as a weapon:[xliv]

How we act – verbally and visually – communicates who we are (in the moment) and influences those around us. It is important to understand what is appropriate, what is in our control, and how our actions can influence, control, and impact others' behaviors.

Of course, there are exceptions to these principles. Individuals can act in a manner unrelated to your behaviors based on mood, experience, beliefs, values, biases, stereotypes, and assumptions. But, following these guidelines may change a toxic environment or a potentially negative interaction into one that is more caring, positive, and respectful.

There's not a chance we'll reach our full potential until we stop blaming each other and start practicing personal accountability. – John Miller, Artist

Practicing Personal Accountability With The QBQ!®

As individuals work to enhance their leaderships skills, they must demonstrate communication effectiveness and accountability. An excellent tool to support these ideals is the QBQ!®.

The QBQ!® stands for The Question Behind the Question, taken from the book, QBQ!® The Question Behind the Question: Practicing Personal Accountability at Work and in Life, by John G. Miller. The QBQ!® provides a framework for personal accountability which, if followed properly, can create a firm foundation for developing the 5-core skills of exceptional leaders.

"The QBQ!® is about practicing personal accountability by asking better questions,"[xlv] and requires a focus on one's choices. Practicing personal accountability requires attention to self without becoming selfish. It requires a focus on "I" to gain a better understanding of others, and a willingness to cooperate and work toward common goals while always asking questions about your role as a change agent and a leader.

The focus on "I" is not ego driven. It is a commitment to personal development, positive engagement, and understanding.

> What can **I do to understand you** better?
> How can **I understand myself** better?
> How can **I understand the needs of the team**?

The QBQ!® places the individual at the center of problem solving and requires honest reflection.

At times in our interactions with others we act instinctually, without being intentional or recognizing the impact of our words, the impact of our actions, and ultimately the impact our behaviors have on our personal and professional reputations. We focus on the task without fully recognizing our individual responsibility to support a successful outcome. The QBQ!® provides a framework for personal accountability and positive action. It is about making better choices in the moment by asking better questions, not necessarily asking questions of others, but asking questions of yourself.

> "How can **I** be more effective?"
> "What can **I** do to meet that deadline?"
> "How can **I** help the team succeed?"[xlvi]

These questions are rooted in personal accountability, problem solving, and a sense of control. Not necessarily control of the situation, but control over the *response* to the situation. The Question Behind the Question is built on the observation that our first reactions are often negative, bringing to mind the "Incorrect Questions, (IQs)"[xlvii] of Why, When, and Who.

- "Why is this happening to me?"[xlviii]
  - When we ask "**Why**?" it can lead to victim thinking and can be stress inducing. We *always* choose our reactions. We choose to act angrily. We choose to shut down our emotions and keep quiet. We choose to worry. Stress is a result of our choices.[xlix]

- "When will someone train me?"[l]
  - When we ask "**When**?" we are really saying we have no choice but to wait and put off action until some point in the future.

- "Who made the mistake?"[li]
  - "**Who**?" focuses on blame and can lead to scapegoating. Blame and "whodunit" questions solve nothing. They create fear, destroy creativity, and build walls.[lii]

If in each moment of decision making, we can discipline our thoughts to look *behind* those initial questions and ask better ones, the questions themselves will lead to better results.

The principles of the QBQ!® focus on asking better questions:

1. Beginning with "What" or "How" (**not** "why," "when," or "who").
2. Containing an "I" (**not** "they," "them," "we," or "you").
3. Focusing on action.[liii]

The spirit of the QBQ!® is personal accountability; it helps remove victim thinking, procrastinating, or blaming, and is built on the recognition that "I can only change me." We must take control of our thoughts and actions especially in the questions we ask when solving problems.

Examples of QBQ!® questions:

- "What can I do today to solve the problem?"
- "How can I help move the project forward?"
- "How can I teach, motivate, and inspire my people to use the tools they have available to do their jobs more effectively?"

Examples of incorrect Questions (IQs):[liv]

- "When will they take care of the problem?"
- "When will someone clarify my job?"
- "When will my staff do what they are supposed to do?"

The QBQ!® allows leaders to practice personal accountability and effective communication, to achieve individual, team, and organizational success.

Behavior And Personal Accountability: A Partnership For Success

One of the most effective ways to succeed at a goal is to have a support network, a mentor, a team, a trusted companion, etc., to coach and support you along the way.

Write down your goal(s) using the principles from "Behavior Breeds Behavior" and the QBQ!® and share them with you support networks.

Remember, your behavior is a critical factor in achieving the success you desire.

My goal(s):
_____
_____
_____
_____
_____
_____
_____
_____

The steps to achieve my goal(s):
_____
_____
_____
_____
_____
_____
_____
_____

What I need from a partner:
_____
_____
_____
_____
_____
_____

Obstacles to success:
_____
_____
_____
_____
_____
_____
_____
_____

Tools to overcome the obstacles:
_____
_____
_____
_____
_____
_____
_____
_____

Notes:
_____
_____
_____
_____
_____
_____
_____

The trouble starts when I fail to notice that I see only whatever confirms my categories and expectations but nothing else. The trouble deepens even further if I kid myself that seeing is believing... — Sue Annis Hammond and Andrea B. Mayfield

Effectively Addressing The Elephant In The Room

One of my favorite books for developing organizational strength and leadership is <u>The Thin Book Of Naming Elephants: How to Surface Undiscussables for Greater Organizational Success,</u> by Sue Annis Hammond and Andrea B. Mayfield. Naming Elephants helps businesses and individuals stop investing in their assumptions and undermining their success.

Naming Elephants is based on lessons learned after the Space Shuttle Columbia accident in 2003. The stated cause of the accident was debris, specifically, foam heat tiles, striking the wing of the craft during liftoff. NASA created an investigative team to review the cause of the accident and discovered that the culture of NASA had as much to do with the accident as the heat tiles.

During the investigation, it was discovered that many lower level staff *believed* that the foam tiles dislodging and striking the craft was potentially dangerous.

Unfortunately, they demonstrated their belief in the following ways:

- They *believed* that if they voiced their concerns they would be fired.
- They *believed* that everyone already knew about the potential hazard.
- They *believed* their own assumptions that since there had not been a serious problem before when foam tiles struck the craft, that there would not be a serious problem now.

When they did voice their beliefs, they were silenced by upper management. In short, the tiles became an elephant that no one discussed, and it led to a tragedy that was potentially avoidable. Hammond and Mayfield describe the *elephant* this way:

1. The elephant stands for all the things no one talks about in an open forum.

2. [Often] the elephant is discussed in an unmanaged and potentially destructive, rather than constructive manner.
3. Not naming elephants can eat away at a person and an organization.[lv]

People learn very quickly that it is better to be quiet than to speak up and look naive, stupid or subversive....[lvi]

In many organizations, there is a gap between what people and the organization say and what people and the organization do. This is called the "Saying/Doing Gap."[lvii] Many organizations are unaware that there is a gap because they do not listen or do not know how to listen to staff concerns.

> The real challenge is to decide which is more destructive: Acknowledging the elephant to deal with it or ignoring it at your organization's peril. – Hammond and Mayfield

There are often "multiple concurrent realities"[lviii] within an organization surrounding mission, goals, and ideas. This is not inherently problematic; it simply means that people can see the same situation, idea, goal, etc., differently. It can be helpful for an organization to see the different ways staff experience the company. It becomes problematic when the voices of difference are silenced or disregarded and/or when disagreement is treated as insubordination. This can stifle creativity and personal investment in the organization.

> We default to the shortcut of 'seeing' things the same way. We stop debating reality.[lix]

This can lead to tunnel vision where we only listen to the voices that we agree with and <u>invest in our own assumptions</u>.

> The trouble starts when I fail to notice that I see only whatever confirms my categories and expectations but nothing else. The trouble deepens even further if I kid myself that seeing is believing... You see what you expect to see. You see what you have the labels to see. You see what you have the skills to manage. Everything else is a blur. And in that 'everything else' lies the developing unexpected event that can bite you and undermine your best intentions.[lx]

There is also the idea that if a problem or issue occurs often enough without significant problems or negative consequences, then the *deviance* or change is okay, and we see it as *normal*. We create new situational and operational *facts*.

This is called the "Normalization of Deviance."[lxi] *Management* believed that the foam strikes were not a risk to the safety of the flight because in the past the foam strikes did not cause significant consequences.

> Facts also develop in a company when someone in a position of power unintentionally creates a fact.[lxii]

When those in positions of power are intolerant of divergent views, discourage organization-wide communication, and do not value dialogue, an atmosphere is created where elephants can thrive. There can be a significant price to having a rigid, inflexible culture; this is called the "Price of Passivity."[lxiii]

Not allowing discussions from all levels effectively places blinders on the company. When this happens, organizations are less likely to see the changing trends in the industry and are slow to respond to the needs of employees and customers.

To foster organizational success, create a culture where people are encouraged to do the following:

- Speak up and share any concerns or ideas.
- Respectfully disagree or agree to disagree.
- Share and debate multiple realities.
- Question those in power.
- Explore many alternatives before shutting down discussions or making decisions.
- Take turns playing devil's advocate or the contrarian.[lxiv]

To begin naming the elephants, leaders must recognize the differences between implicit and explicit communication.

> Everyone talks around the elephant and thinks that everyone else knows about the elephant but until the elephant's presence is made explicit, the level of dialogue – and therefore the quality of decision making – is limited.[lxv]

Naming the elephants is a three-part process:

> **First**, identify what is undiscussable.
> **Second**, surface the underlying assumptions people have about the elephant or the situation.
> **Third**, learn how to have constructive dialogue with the Tops, Middles, and Bottoms.[lxvi]

We need to learn how to discuss the undiscussables by surfacing and addressing our own assumptions and beliefs. We act on our assumptions, which are our "Beliefs about how the world works."[lxvii]

Assumptions are:

- Statements or rules that explain what a person or group generally believes.
- Developed over time and eventually become invisible, or implicit.
- Created out of a human need for stability.[lxviii]

Assumptions are important because they are the "Template through which we view the world."[lxix]

> The longer the assumptions are in effect, and the more success the group [or individual] has, the harder it is for the group [or individual] to see any new information that contradicts its beliefs. [lxx]

To surface and deal with assumptions, we must engage in dialogue.

> ...Constructive dialogue is about people talking to each other in a respectful manner that allows information to be shared and acted on. An environment that respects and expects everyone's unique point of view can be developed through constructive dialogue.[lxxi]

As assumptions are raised and addressed in a constructive way, as the "Tops, Middles, and Bottoms"[lxxii] begin to share information and expose and address elephants, they must begin to execute their mission, goals, and ideals.

> No organization can survive without actually doing what it says it is going to do and holding people accountable.[lxxiii]

The organization and the individuals should do what is expected. This creates "High Reliable Organizations (HROs)."[lxxiv]

> People in High Reliable Organizations are rewarded for pointing out any deviation from the expected.[lxxv]

A High Reliable Organization is always asking questions and listening to the answers; it always endeavors to eliminate the "Saying/Doing Gap." Bridging the saying/doing gap can start small and gain momentum to become the new culture and realized expectation of the company.

Change is personal. It starts with you, the individual, with your commitment to meet the expectations and expose the elephants in a respectful and honest manner.

Organizations are like communities. When all members of the community are connected, the positive changes one person makes may inspire others to follow their example; this is leadership.

Leadership is about understanding the value of relationships, aligning your actions with your beliefs, and taking the time to work with others to help them review their assumptions, find *their* voice in the organization, and expose the elephants that they see.

Leaders must address elephants by creating an organizational culture that recognizes the "Three Universal Human Needs"[lxxvi] as defined by Dr. David Cooperrider. Each person needs to:

1. Have a voice and be heard;
2. Be viewed as essential to a group; and
3. Be seen as unique and exceptional.[lxxvii]

With these ideas in action, leaders, and the organizations they work with, can create environments free of elephants and remove significant roadblocks to success.

CHAPTER THREE

DISTINCTIVE QUALITIES OF LEADERS

If you want to be trusted be trustworthy. — Stephen Covey

DISTINCTIVE QUALITIES OF LEADERS

Leaders Are Trustworthy

Merriam Webster defines trust as, "Assured reliance on the character, ability, strength, or truth of someone or something; belief that someone or something is reliable, good, honest, effective, etc."[lxxviii]

There are those who believe that one's title automatically engenders trust. That is a fallacy. Having the title of CFO, COO, Owner, President, Director, Manager, Supervisor, etc., does not make you trustworthy, just as having those titles does not mean that you deserve respect. Trust and respect are always earned and no title, perks, false promises, (perceived) power, entitlement, or platitudes will force someone to trust you.

How you treat others, how you engage with your colleagues, employees, and customers ultimately determines trustworthiness. Employees want to work for a company they can *trust*, one that is stable, innovative, and engages with them in an honest and respectful manner. Employers want talented people they can *trust* to deliver on the promise of the brand, create consistency in their products, and ensure customer loyalty.

In the article How Workplace Culture Can Attract the Right Employees, Rosemary Bryant, a Director of Human Capital Consulting with TriNet, frames the idea of trustworthiness in the context of company culture to attract and retain employees:

> Strong potential employees don't really care about ping pong tables or free lunches when it comes to choosing their next career move. The employees you want are interested in a work environment that will enable them to grow their careers, provide greater satisfaction and give them the experiences that make work worthwhile. This type of culture is harder to find than 401K matching or free pizza in the breakroom. Culture creates the type of commitment you want from great employees. Culture is the key differentiator that sets you apart and ultimately forms the competitive landscape. [lxxix]

Creating a work culture that allows employees to "grow their careers, provide greater satisfaction and give them the experiences that make work worthwhile;" in essence, allowing employees to thrive, is only possible with a foundation of trust.

- Trust is the glue of life. It's the most essential ingredient in effective communication. It's the foundational principle that holds all relationships. – *Stephen Covey*
- Leaders must exemplify integrity and earn the trust of their teams through their everyday actions. When you do this, you set high standards for everyone at your company. And when you do so with positive energy and enthusiasm for shared goals and purpose, you can deeply connect with your team and customers. – *Marillyn Hewson*
- The toughest thing about the power of trust is that it's very difficult to build and very easy to destroy. The essence of trust building is to emphasize the similarities between you and the customer. – *Thomas J. Watson*
- Trust is more important than ever to our lives and businesses. It requires that leaders view those they work with as whole and complete beings, not as 'human resources'. – *Jayne Warrilow*
- Creating a high trust culture is exactly where being a positive force for good and high performance coincides. Trust cannot be ignored by any leader because without it there is no leadership. – *Andrea Reibmayr*
- If you don't have trust inside your company, then you can't transfer it to your customers. – *Roger Staubach*

What consistently gets in the way of building trust? It is **always** behavior. A constant theme in my articles and training sessions is the concept of living by your values – whether they are organizational or individual values.

- Values [are] important and enduring beliefs or ideals shared by the members of a culture about what is good or desirable and what is not. Values exert major influence on the behavior of an individual and serve as broad guidelines in all situations.[lxxx]
- Values can be defined as broad preferences concerning appropriate courses of action or outcomes. As such, values reflect a person's sense of right and wrong or what "ought" to be. …Values tend to influence attitudes and behavior.[lxxxi]

Values are <u>always</u> demonstrated through behaviors. If you behave in a manner that engenders trust – whether you are an organization or an individual – you will be seen as trustworthy. This is the one trait that separates good leaders from great leaders.

Unfortunately, many leaders and companies have what can best be described as "Fluctuating Values" based on mood, the moment, the campaign, the crowd, or potential profits. This is most dramatically displayed during an election season. Many politicians change their messages based on their audience and the time of year, often being a firebrand for their base only to pivot as they speak to the larger general population. They espouse different *values* in the hopes of winning votes.

Fluctuating values in business, politics, or personal relationships undermines trust and should be seen for what it is – disingenuous and trust destroying.

One of the greatest challenges for leaders and organizations is to consistently deliver what they promise. Not living up to our promises undermines trust. This is true in business, politics, and all aspects of life.

Being trustworthy literally means being *worthy* of the trust someone invests in you. Do not let mood, money, fame, or power undermine your values – be trustworthy - period.

Top 10 ways to earn trust:

1. Be trustworthy. Act in a manner worthy of trust. Actions speak much louder than words.
2. Treat people fairly.
3. Communicate effectively.
4. Share your knowledge, experience, and time.
5. Say thank you.
6. Treat people with respect.
7. Acknowledge the achievements and contributions of others.
8. Reward success.
9. Know your people. A good leader knows the skills, strengths, and weaknesses of their team members and how to best support them.
10. Do not hide your mistakes. Acknowledge them, ask for help, and find ways to fix them.

Top 10 ways to lose trust:

1. Being dishonest.
2. Disengaging or not engaging with others.
3. Being a bully or abusing your power or title.
4. Being disrespectful.
5. Making sure people "know their place." Treating people as objects or as if they are expendable.
6. Taking credit for the work of others and/or not recognizing the contributions of others.
7. Undermining someone's character, accomplishments, etc.
8. Berating people in public or private.
9. Ignoring your employees' or colleagues' needs.
10. Not communicating effectively.

Characteristics Of Trustworthiness

Being trustworthy is a defining quality of character. Earning the trust of others is the ultimate sign of respect and a true testament to leadership.

Choose ten (10) characteristics of trustworthiness for yourself. Reflect on the answers and evaluate if your behaviors support your checked choices. Share <u>The Characteristics of Trustworthiness Checklist</u> with your colleagues and teams. Compile the top ten (10) responses from all members of your teams. Discuss the results, the consistent answers and the outliers, and develop an action plan to align the individual values of trustworthiness with the values of the organization. Engage in the behaviors necessary to demonstrate that the characteristics are more than just words.

- ☐ Trusts others.
- ☐ Follows through on commitments.
- ☐ Maintains confidence.
- ☐ Directly addresses individuals with whom there is conflict rather than telling uninvolved parties.
- ☐ Listens respectfully.
- ☐ Accepts others without judgment or question.
- ☐ Performs responsibilities with quality and timeliness.
- ☐ Seeks out and considers opposing viewpoints.
- ☐ Behaves consistently and predictably over time.
- ☐ Acts in a way that matches expressed values, beliefs, and priorities (walks the talk).
- ☐ Openly expresses goals, intentions, and priorities.
- ☐ Shares information.
- ☐ Shows respect for others' viewpoints during disagreements.
- ☐ Evaluates plans and ideas in an objective, logical fashion.
- ☐ Demonstrates sensitivity and tact.
- ☐ Involves others in problem solving and decision making.
- ☐ Communicates clearly to minimize misunderstanding.
- ☐ Works to solve problems rather than assign blame.
- ☐ Gives recognition and credit to others when warranted.
- ☐ Encourages the open discussion of problems and differences of opinion.
- ☐ Values input from others regardless of position.
- ☐ Is collaborative.
- ☐ Admits mistakes.
- ☐ Approaches conflict with an open mind and a desire for respectful resolution.
- ☐ Remains non-defensive when met with disagreement.
- ☐ Requests help when needed.
- ☐ Takes interpersonal risks when appropriate.

In looking for people to hire, you look for three qualities: integrity, intelligence, and energy. And if they don't have the first, the other two will kill you. —
Warren Buffet

Leaders Are Ethical

During a discussion on supporting organizational mission statements and business ethics, a staff member stated that the only responsibility any business or employee has is to enhance the bottom line of the company – profit – regardless of their individual values or the company's mission statement. They punctuated this belief with the comment, "Who cares about your mission statement if you aren't making money?" Yikes!!!

Profit cannot be the only factor in determining success. There are a host of failed companies that believed *profit-above-all-else* was the only real "Business Ethic."

We lamented the fact that for some, personal ethics seemed to take a back seat to business ethics. After the conversation ended, one of the participants sent me the following commentary from Michael Josephson, of the Josephson Institute of Ethics:

> There's No Such Thing as Business Ethics 343:1
>
> Some years ago, a senior executive at a Fortune 100 company objected when I asserted that corporations have an ethical, as well as a legal obligation to keep promises and honor their contracts. He said that the decision to live up to or ignore contractual commitments is a business decision, not an ethical one. The other party has legal remedies, he said, and therefore responsible managers have a duty to evaluate whether it's in the company's best interest to honor or breach contracts. The decision should be based on a simple cost/benefit analysis. Ethics has nothing to do with it.
>
> Disturbingly common, this claim of moral immunity is based on the erroneous idea that in business the only thing to consider is self-interest. The theory that expediency, not ethics, should control decision making flourishes because many people compartmentalize their lives into personal and business domains, assuming each is governed by

different standards of ethics.

In business, the argument goes, ethical principles are simply factors to be taken into account; they're not moral obligations. As a result, fundamentally good people who would never lie, cheat or break a promise in their personal lives delude themselves into thinking that they can properly do so in business.

Nonsense! There's no such thing as "business ethics" -- there's only ethics. Fundamental standards of right and wrong like trustworthiness, respect, responsibility, fairness, caring and good citizenship do not become irrelevant when we enter the workplace. And it doesn't matter how many people think otherwise. Remember, ethics is not a description of the way people actually behave. It's a prescription for how they ought to behave.

This is Michael Josephson reminding you that character counts.[lxxxii]

Mission statements offer a window into the values of an organization. How an organization behaves – its actions - outweigh any slogans or declarations it makes. Therefore, mission statements should be more than just platitudes. They should establish the values and ideals of the organization and serve as the foundation for how all members of the organization will act.

Patrick Hull, a contributor to Forbes, states that there are four essential questions that a mission statement must answer:

- What do we do?
- How do we do it?
- Whom do we do it for?
- What value are we bringing?[lxxxiii]

When you use words like integrity, excellence, customer focused, honest, caring, etc., to describe your business, these words should also mean that your personal values - demonstrated through behaviors - are aligned and that you will act in an appropriate and ethical manner.

As Michael Josephson states, there is no such thing as "business ethics" – there is only ethics.

Thankfulness sets in motion a chain reaction that transforms all around us... including ourselves. For no one ever misunderstands the melody of a grateful heart. Its message is universal; its lyrics transcend all earthly barriers; its music touches the heavens. — Anonymous

Leaders Are Thankful

Each one of us should take time to reflect on what we are thankful for – no matter how small. Every success, every obstacle overcome, provides an opportunity to be thankful.

With so much negativity in the world we can sometimes forget to be thankful for what truly matters; our well-being, family, friends, and those special moments that rekindle our spirit and remind us that there is peace, love, and goodness in this world.

> We can only be said to be alive in those moments when our hearts are conscious of our treasures. – Thornton Wilder

When we are inundated with negativity, we begin to believe that disappointment, problems, tragedy, and disaster are the only constants in this world. Let us combat that belief by appreciating the positive. Every day there are countless acts of heroism and positivity as well as moments of happiness, joy, peace, and goodness.

I would challenge us all to pay attention to the good, the fun, and the pleasant moments. Take a tally of the smiles and the laughter and recognize that these moments happen more often than we realize. I would challenge us all to pay attention to everything that happens in our lives – not just the negative – and live with a sense of gratitude.

> Gratitude unlocks the fullness of life. It turns what we have into enough, and more. It turns denial into acceptance, chaos to order, confusion to clarity. It can turn a meal into a feast, a house into a home, a stranger into a friend. Gratitude makes sense of our past,

> brings peace for today and creates a vision for tomorrow. –
> Melody Beattie

We should think about the opportunities we have to give something, no matter how small, to others. Whether it is a warm greeting, a smile, your time, your finances, or your attention, we all can positively impact others and be the change we want to see.

> Not what we say about our blessings, but how we use them, is
> the true measure of our thanksgiving. – WT Purkiser

Hope will never be silent. — Harvey Milk

Leaders Are Hopeful

As we reflect on the acts of violence impacting so many communities, we must not become consumed searching for "reason" or a deeper "understanding" of terrorist acts. Deliberate acts of mass violence cannot be understood as "reasonable." The focus of terrorism is to incite fear, undermine our sense of safety, and destroy hope.

The perpetrators always provide their rationale or their manifesto, but their excuses for violence are inexcusable and defy reason.

In the face of indefensible violence, we can expect moments of silence, a reaffirmation of inter-governmental cooperation, increased security measures, and heightened vigilance… Unfortunately, we can also expect a heightened sense of individual anxiety and personal vulnerability.

These feelings are understandable as our sense of comfort and safety are shattered. Conflict, violence, war, terrorism, all cause despair.

Do not lose hope.

We are resilient. No matter the tragedy, the ability for the human spirit to persevere, survive, and flourish is undeniable.

Do not lose hope.

This is more than a cliché. Hope is the essence of the human condition and is part of our DNA. Hope is what drives ordinary people to act with heroism and compassion; to put their own safety at risk to help a stranger. Hope is what allows people of disparate nations to unite across borders and recognize their common bonds. Hope allows us to take the actions necessary to survive in the worst of times, through the most heinous circumstances, to stand and face the horrors of the world, and not lose our humanity, dignity, or compassion.

Pain, sorrow, and anger are real and justified. *Do not lose hope.*

In the face of war, tragedy, and personal pain many of our leaders have recognized the power of hope:

- Hope is being able to see that there is light despite all of the darkness. – Desmond Tutu
- We have always held to the hope, the belief, the conviction that there is a better life, a better world, beyond the horizon. – Franklin D. Roosevelt
- Optimism is the faith that leads to achievement. Nothing can be done without hope and confidence. – Helen Keller
- Our uniqueness, our individuality, and our life experience molds us into fascinating beings. I hope we can embrace that. I pray we may all challenge ourselves to delve into the deepest resources of our hearts to cultivate an atmosphere of understanding, acceptance, tolerance, and compassion. We are all in this life together. – Linda Thompson
- Faith is not simply a patience that passively suffers until the storm is past. Rather, it is a spirit that bears things - with resignations, yes, but above all, with blazing, serene hope. – Corazon Aquino

Hope is not the same as a wish. A wish requires no action except for the energy necessary to create the wish. Hope requires action, perseverance, and commitment. Hope requires that you have a vision of what you want your life and the world you live in to be – and then work to make that happen.

Hope is action.

If we hope for a better future, we need to work to create that future. If we hope for a world where there are no acts of senseless violence, then we must work toward that end.

Leaders **hope** for peace – Leaders **work** for peace.

Our thoughts and prayers should be with all who suffer from natural disasters, war, violence, poverty, displacement, and pain. No matter what happens – do not lose hope.

> Hope is the thing with feathers that perches in the soul - and sings the tunes without the words - and never stops at all. – Emily Dickinson

Every great dream begins with a dreamer. Always remember, you have within you the strength, the patience, and the passion to reach for the stars to change the world. — Harriet Tubman

Leaders Are Dreamers

I was walking in downtown Los Angeles when a sign in a window caught my eye.

IF YOU DON'T BUILD YOUR DREAM,
SOMEONE WILL HIRE YOU TO BUILD THEIRS.

I stood there for a minute, pulled out my phone, and snapped a picture. As I walked away, I had several thoughts.

What happened to our dreams; the ones we had when we were young and had no limitations? What happened to our grand ideas of saving the world, or being firefighters or astronauts; of finding cures for diseases with names we could not pronounce; of being rock stars, discovering ancient civilizations, or finding hidden treasure at the bottom of the ocean? What happened to our dreams?

For many of us we got tired, disenchanted, or did not want to do the work to make our dreams a reality. We became *reasonable, practical,* or *realistic*; we *grew up* and forgot that our dreams filled us with joy, motivation, and hope. We forgot that we once started every conversation with "what if" and "someday I will," and "when I grow up, I'm going to be…" Having dreams used to be cool.

Many of us think that our dreams abandoned us… but I think we abandoned our dreams. We grew tired when our dreams did not come true and stopped believing in magic.

Keep Dreaming.

Your dreams bring you joy and happiness, and they can still come true. The proof is all around us. In 2015 a new species of extinct hominin, Homo Naledi, was identified; discovered by *recreational cavers*. The Rare Genomics Institute helps to accelerate some of the most substantial genetic research to date, and they are an *all-volunteer* organization. A family of treasure hunters found a million dollars in gold coins in a 300-year-old shipwreck, 15 feet below the ocean's surface. Dreams still come true.

Build your dreams and joy will follow.

1. Dreams are the seeds of change. Nothing ever grows without a seed, and nothing ever changes without a dream. – Debby Boone
2. A goal is a dream with a deadline. – Napoleon Hill
3. To accomplish great things, we must not only act, but also dream; not only plan, but also believe. – Anatole France
4. Hold fast to dreams, for if dreams die, life is a broken-winged bird that cannot fly. – Langston Hughes
5. Without leaps of imagination, or dreaming, we lose the excitement of possibilities. Dreaming, after all, is a form of planning. – Gloria Steinem
6. When you stop having dreams and ideals -- well, you might as well stop altogether. – Marian Anderson
7. Dreams are renewable. No matter what our age or condition, there are still untapped possibilities within us and new beauty waiting to be born. – Dale Turner
8. Cherish your visions and your dreams as they are the children of your soul, the blueprints of your ultimate achievements. – Napoleon Hill
9. Without dreams, there can be no courage. And without courage, there can be no action. – Wim Wenders
10. Dreams pass into the reality of action. From the actions stems the dream again; and this interdependence produces the highest form of living. – Anais Nin

In real life, the most practical advice for leaders is not to treat pawns like pawns, nor princes like princes, but all persons like persons. — James MacGregor Burns

Leaders Listen And Provide Actionable Advice

Opinions can be offered by anyone, regardless of skill, experience, or knowledge of the subject matter. A leader's reputation depends on the information they provide. It is imperative to offer sound actionable advice that informs, supports, and enhances individual and organizational needs.

Below are six (6) keys to providing sound actionable A.D.V.I.C.E.:

- A – Be **Accountable**
- D – Have **Drive**
- V – Support the organizational **Values**
- I – Demonstrate **Integrity**
- C – **Communicate** effectively
- E – Prove your **Execution** skills

A – Accountability. The information one provides should come from experience, knowledge, and an understanding of the facts. Markets, laws, and times change. Leaders must stay up-to-date and be accountable for the information they present. In my opinion, the best definition of accountability comes from the book The Oz Principle, by Roger Connors, Tom Smith, and Craig Hickman. Accountability is "A personal choice to rise above one's circumstances and demonstrate the ownership necessary for achieving Key Results; to See It,® Own It, ® Solve It,® and Do It.®"[lxxxiv] Following this definition of accountability requires a personal commitment to doing what it takes to meet your clients' needs.

D – Drive. Being passionate about something is not the same as being driven. Passion can be a visceral and intensely emotional behavior that can defy rational thought and action. This can lead to poor decision making. Being driven requires emotional intensity <u>and</u> thoughtful deliberate action, focused on achieving specific outcomes. The Oxford Dictionary defines drive as "an organized effort to achieve a goal."[lxxxv] Leaders should understand the difference between passion and drive.

V – Values. The beliefs and behaviors that *drive* an individual or an organization. Values are the foundation on which individuals and organizations act. They are the core beliefs that inform all that we do and define character. Understanding your personal values as well as the values of the individuals or organizations you support is necessary to offer sound actionable advice.

I – Integrity. The Free Dictionary defines integrity as "Uncompromising adherence to moral and ethical principles; soundness of moral character; honesty."[lxxxvi] Integrity is connected to individual and organizational values demonstrated by behaviors and is exemplified in the following quote by Dr. Larry Roper, "There is no such thing as an unimportant or insignificant relationship…"[lxxxvii] How we treat others, our actions – not just our words – demonstrate a commitment to integrity.

C – Communication. The act of expressing or exchanging information, ideas, thoughts, feelings, etc., to someone else and having the information received and understood in the way that was intended. The concept of communication seems so simple – share information with others – but communication is truly a minefield. We need to focus on <u>effective</u> communication when offering sound and actionable advice. Effective communication is enhanced by practicing the *nine (9) essential skills for facilitation* discussed in chapter two:

1. Validate someone's experience.
2. Listen without judgment – bracketing judgments.
3. Synthesize information.
4. Help someone rephrase a question/statement for clarity and understanding.
5. Ask questions without bringing in judgments.
6. Identify and challenge assumptions.
7. Challenge a statement without de-valuing the person.
8. Provide information/teach while maintaining collegiality (peership).
9. Recognize the teachable moments.

E – Execution. Simply put, execution is the process of completing a task. Unfortunately, execution can be one of the most difficult processes an organization or a leader may face. Larry Bossidy and Ram Charan, in their book <u>Execution: The Discipline of Getting Things Done</u>, define execution as "A systematic way of exposing reality and acting on it."[lxxxviii]

Execution requires finding the answers to six (6) questions:

1. Which people will do the job?
2. How will they be held accountable?
3. What resources are needed to execute the strategy?
4. What are the future resource needs of the organization?
5. Does the strategy deliver the earnings to be successful?
6. Can it be broken down into doable initiatives?[lxxxix]

Bossidy and Charan believe, "The heart of execution lies in three core processes: the <u>people</u> process, the <u>strategy</u> process, and the <u>operations</u> process."[xc] They also believe that "the intellectual challenge of execution is getting to the heart of an issue through persistent and constructive probing."[xci]

Answering questions and offering opinions is simple, but providing sound actionable advice requires a commitment to the six (6) keys: **A**ccountability, **D**rive, **V**alues, **I**ntegrity, **C**ommunication, and **E**xecution.

You can look for external sources of motivation and that can catalyze a change, but it won't sustain one. It has to be from an internal desire. — Jillian Michaels

Leaders Provide Motivation

Paula Abdul is credited with saying, "Everyone is your best friend when you are successful. Make sure that the people that you surround yourself with are also the people that you are not afraid of failing with."

This is sound advice from someone who has experienced the ups and downs of business success.

I'm always interested in a good motivational quote, especially when it is applicable to personal life, business, and sports. But, so many "good quotes" leave us hanging. One of the best known, "Just Do It," is a great motto and can be inspirational, but it lacks a critical detail – *how to do it*.

It is easy to say, "Just do it;" "kick the ball into the goal," or "work harder than your competition," but a good quote offers something more, direction, instruction, an explanation on how to do it, or at least a statement as to why *doing it* is important.

I am just as interested in the *how to*, (the explanation) as I am in the *Just do*, (the motivation). Some might say "Dude, you're asking for too much, it's just a quote, not a business course," others might say "it's not even a quote, it's a slogan," but I hear respected leaders saying "Just do it" in meetings and at sporting events often enough to know that it is used as a motivational quote. Do not get me wrong, I think "Just do it" is a great statement – it motivates and compels one to action – but I also think a good quote can inspire or motivate <u>and</u> inform or explain at the same time.

Paula's quote is a great example of the balance of these two ideas. The first part of her quote offers the *Just do it* statement; the information, engagement, or motivational piece – "Everyone is your best friend when you are successful."

The second part of the quote is the *How to do it* or *What to do about it* statement; the explanation, the how, and why this is relevant – "Make sure that the people that you surround yourself with are also the people that you are not afraid of failing with."

I think the best motivational quotes incorporate both pieces in their statements.

In sports or business, it is easy to make the "Just Do It" statement as a motivator, but as the parent of kids who play sports, I am interested in a little more substance. I want a leader, not just a coach.

I have watched countless parents and coaches yell and repeat "Just do it!" as the technique of choice when trying to motivate their players. I have never found this helpful. Successful leaders in sports and in business demonstrate skill, enthusiasm, drive, knowledge, the ability to successfully share information (*effective communication*), and lots of patience.

Good leaders in sports and business are just as interested in the "How to" as they are in the "Just do." The best leaders stop the practice and show the players *how to* do what is being asked of them; how to turn the foot just right so that the ball goes where they want it to go. A good leader in business provides the words of encouragement and the tools to help direct the business.

As part of Nike's 30th anniversary celebration of the "Just Do It" campaign, the company unveiled an addendum to their slogan:

>"Believe in something. Even if it means sacrificing everything."

This quote meets the standard for being well-rounded. Gino Fisanotti, Nike's Vice President of Brand for North America, explained the decision to feature Colin Kaepernick and update their slogan this way, "We believe Colin is one of the most inspirational athletes of this generation, who has leveraged the power of sport to help move the world forward…We wanted to energize its meaning and introduce 'Just Do It' to a new generation of athletes"[xcii]

Good leaders assess needs, provide tools, and support the actions that drive success. Good quotes do the same.

My top 10 Motivational and Instructional Quotes:

1. There are no secrets to success. It is the result of preparation, hard work, and learning from failure. – Colin Powell

2. You can buy a person's time; you can buy their physical presence at a given place; you can even buy a measured number of their skilled muscular motions per hour. But you can not buy enthusiasm... you can not buy loyalty. You can not buy the devotion of hearts, minds, or souls. You must earn these. – Clarence Francis

3. Clients do not come first. Employees come first. If you take care of your employees, they will take care of the clients. – Sir Richard Branson

4. Nothing in the World can take the place of persistence. Talent will not; nothing is more common than unsuccessful men with talent. Genius will not; unrewarded genius is almost a proverb. Education will not; the world is full of educated derelicts. Persistence and determination are omnipotent. The slogan 'press on' has solved and always will solve the problems of the human race. – Calvin Coolidge

5. All that is necessary to break the spell of inertia and frustration is this: Act as if it were impossible to fail. That is the talisman, the formula, the command of right-about-face which turns us from failure towards success. – Dorothea Brande

6. Remind yourself regularly that you are better than you think you are. Successful people are not superhuman. Success does not require a super-intellect. Nor is there anything mystical about success. And success isn't based on luck. Successful people are just ordinary folks who have developed belief in themselves and what they do. Never -- yes, never -- sell yourself short. – David J. Schwartz

7. I didn't get there by wishing for it or hoping for it, but by working for it. – Estee Lauder

8. There is no royal flower-strewn path to success. And if there is, I have not found it for if I have accomplished anything in life it is because I have been willing to work hard. – Madam C.J. Walker

9. If you are committed to creating value and if you aren't afraid of hard times; obstacles become utterly unimportant. A nuisance perhaps; but with no real power. The world respects creation; people will get out of your way. – Candice Carpenter

10. If you think you're beaten, you are;
    If you think you dare not, you don't;
    If you'd like to win, but think, you can't
    It's almost a cinch you won't.
    If you think you will lose, you're lost;

For out in the world we find,
Success begins with a fellow's will,
It's all in the state of mind.

If you think you're outclassed, you are;
You've got to think high to rise.
You've got to hustle before
You can ever win a prize.
Life's battles don't always go
To the stronger or faster man,
But sooner or later the man who wins
Is the one who thinks he can. – Walter D. Wintle

(*Okay, I know this last one is a poem not a quote…but it is a great motivator.*)

There are seven things that will destroy us: Wealth without work; Pleasure without conscience; Knowledge without character; Religion without sacrifice; Politics without principle; Science without humanity; Business without ethics. — Mahatma Gandhi

Leaders Must Raise The Bar On Personal Accountability Or Face The Death Of Responsibility

Every four years the United States engages in the process of electing a new president. The process can be a withering display of stamina, hyperbole, and callousness. The 2016 election season took callousness and vitriol to new heights, with demonstrations of denial and obfuscation from politicians who seemed immune to the concept of accepting or admitting responsibility for their actions or demonstrating a contrite heart.

It seemed for some, that the very act of saying "I'm sorry," "I was wrong," "my actions were not right," or any other straightforward admission of personal responsibility was anathema. Instead of offering apologies, there was a focus on damage control. Instead of contrition and honest reflection, there was blame, distraction, and a pivot away from personal responsibility. Many of these same behaviors were present in the 2018 midterm elections as well.

Is this the new normal? Is personal responsibility dead?

The fallout from the statements and actions of the candidates and their surrogates may have a negative effect on the political process and civil discourse for years to come.

This "death of responsibility" is not limited to US politicians; Boris Johnson, Rodrigo Duterte, Vladimir Putin, and leaders in Honduras, Syria, Nigeria, Brazil, Venezuela, Ethiopia, etc., have made statements and engaged in behaviors where the death of responsibility seems to reign supreme.

Acting responsibly should be an ethical imperative for leaders.

> Success in leadership is not achieved by standing on the necks of others or by destroying your reputation or the reputation of others, but by connecting with a set of positive guiding principles and working diligently in an ethical and positive manner to achieve results. Success

and leadership require a dedication to responsible behavior that many of our 'successful leaders' lack.[xciii]

Responsibility in leadership requires a demonstration of principles, including tact, truthfulness, and accountability for one's words and deeds. Unfortunately, during political seasons we typically see the absence of these values.

> The most practical kind of politics is the politics of decency. - Theodore Roosevelt

I am sure that many will say that our leaders, especially political leaders, engage in falsehoods and halfhearted apologies as a matter of course. But I refuse to accept this as a necessity, not because I am naïve or confused about human nature or politics, but because I believe our leaders can make better choices based on higher principles and still be successful.

> I am different from [George] Washington; I have a higher, grander standard of principle. Washington could not lie. I can lie, but I won't. - Mark Twain

Intentional misstatements and halfhearted apologies are insulting. Dishonest behaviors undermine character and lead to cynicism, mistrust, and a lack of faith in the people and the systems designed to serve the public. The result is the death of responsibility.

Should we accept this death as the new normal? Should we shrug off the insults and despotic behaviors as the reality of politics and corporations?

NO.

> There are seasons in every country when noise and impudence pass current for worth; and in popular commotions especially, the clamors of interested and factious men are often mistaken for patriotism. - Alexander Hamilton

We can and should demand more from those in power, <u>not</u> perfection, but competence, decency, contrition, and proof of promises, and then hold them accountable when they break their word or go off course.

When corporate leaders like those from Wells Fargo and Fox engage in fraud or harassment and then retire with multi-million-dollar severance packages, there is a confirmation that those in power play by a different set of rules.

But, even in business, responsibility and integrity matter:

> We need to stress that personal integrity is as important as executive skill in business dealings.... Setting an example from the top has a ripple effect throughout a business school or a corporation. After nearly three decades in business, 10 years as chief executive of a Big Eight accounting firm, I have learned that the standards set at the top filter throughout a company.... [Quoting Professor Thomas Dunfee of the Wharton School:] ' A company that fails to take steps to produce a climate conducive to positive work-related ethical attitudes may create a vacuum in which employees so predisposed may foster a frontier-style, everyone for themselves mentality.' - Russell E. Palmer

When our leaders engage in behaviors that are offensive, abominable, appalling, shocking, and ugly, but then simply deny their actions or state that their words were taken out of context, they should be held accountable and be reminded that accepting responsibility for one's actions is a sign of leadership.

> As a leader, you have to not only do the right thing, but be perceived to be doing the right thing. A consequence of seeking a leadership position is being put under intense public scrutiny, being held to high standards, and enhancing a reputation that is constantly under threat. – Firing Back, by Jeffrey Sonnenfeld and Andrew Ward

Accountability leads to redemption. Addressing concerns honestly demonstrates integrity and is the first step in rebuilding one's character.

> Trust is rebuilt by focusing not on what the other person did or did not do but on critiquing one's *own* behavior, improving one's trustworthiness, and focusing attention not on words and promises but on actions, attitudes, and ways of being. – The Art of Waking People Up, by Kenneth Cloke and Joan Goldsmith

> Re-examine all that you have been told . . . dismiss that which insults your soul. – Walt Whitman

To avoid the death of responsibility we should **R.A.I.S.E.** the bar on personal accountability for ourselves and our leaders.

- **Recognize** your actions.
- **Accept** responsibility.
- **Initiate** an appropriate response to address or fix the mistake(s).
- **Support** those impacted by the mistake(s).
- **Evolve** and change your patterns of behavior.

For our political and corporate leaders, the public does not ask for perfection but does seek consistency without pretense. We want leaders to do what is right, not what is expedient. We seek leadership demonstrated by character, integrity, and responsibility. **R.A.I.S.E.** the bar and ensure that personal responsibility is not dead.

> Always do right. This will gratify some people and astonish the rest. – Mark Twain

The only thing you sometimes have control over is perspective. You don't have control over your situation. But you have a choice about how you view it. — Chris Pine

Leaders Maintain Perspective Through Tough Times

Lately, paying attention to any news source can be an exercise in controlled terror; wildfires, hurricanes, mass shootings, earthquakes, migrant deaths and deportations, emboldened white supremacist, terrorism, political unrest, unaccountable politicians, war, famine, and suffering around the world. We see so much negativity and pain that we can become desensitized to the horrors of the world or tune out altogether.

We seem to be drawn to bad news and the maxim, "If it bleeds, it leads." Jacob Burak, in his article <u>Humans are wired for bad news, angry faces and sad memories. Is this negativity bias useful or something to overcome?</u>[xciv] states that "Negative events affect us more than positive ones. We remember them more vividly and they play a larger role in shaping our lives."

Peter H. Diamandis and Steven Kotler, in their book <u>Abundance: The Future is Better Than You Think</u>, address this same issue:

> These are turbulent times. A quick glance at the headlines is enough to set anybody on edge and – with the endless media stream that has become our lives – it's hard to get away from the headlines. Worse, evolution shaped the human brain to be acutely aware of all potential dangers…it literally shuts off our ability to take in good news.[xcv]

There will always be bad news, the world is a dangerous place, but that does not mean that our awareness of danger or our experience with pain and suffering excludes, diminishes, or undermines our ability to enjoy those moments of beauty, happiness, love, peace, and joy.

Diamandis and Kotler explain their idea that humans are hardwired for bad news as a function of survival connected to our "fight-or-flight" instinct. This response or reflex is rooted in a concept called "Negativity Bias." The theory is that negative experiences have a greater impact on our behaviors, thoughts, and feelings than something positive because they provide important lessons on safety, security, and survival.

Negativity bias may have been necessary for our ancestors to survive in the wild, but we have transferred the dangers of the natural world into all aspects of our lives, including our business and personal relationships. We are so attuned to negativity that it can take a superhuman effort for us to recognize the positive experiences in our lives.

In Abundance, the authors cite Zoologist Matt Ridley's comments addressing the pervasive nature of negativity bias:

> "It's incredible," he says, "this moaning pessimism, this knee-jerk, things-are-going-downhill reaction from people living amid luxury and security that their ancestors would have died for. The tendency to see the emptiness of every glass is pervasive. It's almost as if people cling to bad news like a comfort blanket."[xcvi]

Thankfully, the authors also share the remedy to overcome our hardwired instincts toward the negative – receiving praise. We need positive reinforcement.

Jacob Burak describes the importance of receiving praise in our professional and personal lives:

> …couples needed a 'magic ratio' of at least five positive expressions for each negative one if a relationship was to survive.
>
> …In the most effective groups, employees were praised six times for every time they were put down.[xcvii]

He also describes the formula to beat negativity bias:

> …'critical positivity ratio'…devised the perfect formula of 3-6:1. In other words, hearing praise between three and six times as often as criticism, the researchers said, sustained employee satisfaction, success in love, and most other measures of a flourishing, happy life.[xcviii]

Receiving praise is important in all aspects of our lives. Unfortunately, all too often we create negative self-fulfilling prophecies within our relationships, building roadblocks to success with our thoughts and behaviors. We offer negative reinforcement to those around us, focusing solely on what is not working – the bad news. We are so invested in negativity bias that we see bad news and failure as inevitable. This anticipation of failure can keep us from investing in or creating meaningful and lasting relationships.

Incidents in life can be devastating. I have experienced enough pain and loss to know this to be a fact, and I have no pretense that the world holds me in high esteem. But I also do not see the world as being out to get me. *People* yes, the *world*, no. It is important to learn to live without the constant fear that negativity bias creates. This means that we must fight against our most basic instincts and live a life of possibilities and promise, not anxiety, worry, or dread.

Please do not misinterpret this statement and believe that I want everyone to move through life wearing blinders, believing only in the inherent goodness in people; that would be naïve and dangerous. But I do believe in balance, perspective, hope, and an overriding sense that everyone deserves happiness, beauty, and joy in their life.

I believe that all leaders should look for the magic moment in all things, whether it is the magical opening of traffic on the 405 freeway, the arrival of a half-full subway car at 14th Street and Union Square, the beauty of a sunrise or sunset, or that moment of quiet before the storm.

Do not disregard these moments simply because they are short-lived or infrequent. Honor them, believe that it is okay to enjoy life, and embrace a balanced perspective.

I offer a reminder of a greater vision of the world we live in. It is a reminder in the power of Hope. Not to put a smiley face on pain and suffering, but as a reminder of life in balance.

Hope is kindness in action, offering positive reinforcement and praise in a world where those behaviors seem foreign. Hope is demonstrated through acts of caring. Hope is what defeats negativity bias.

> Leaders maintain perspective through tough times.

In the long run, we shape our lives, and we shape ourselves. The process never ends until we die. And the choices we make are ultimately our own responsibility. – Eleanor Roosevelt

Leaders Recognize The Impact Of Their Choices

I walked in on a conversation where staff members were discussing business ethics as demonstrated by the participants on a reality TV show.

The conversation centered around the idea of trust, specifically, if someone would make a good employee if they were willing to do *anything* to get the job. Some of the staff members thought the participants on the show were simply playing a role on-screen and would not demonstrate those same characteristics when the cameras were turned off.

My views are clear, do not sacrifice your integrity or character for 15-minutes of fame. There should not be an on/off switch for values. Manipulators and rationalizers do not make good employees. They tend to search for excuses rather than solutions and make poor choices when it comes to building trust.

Choice can be defined as the opportunity or power to decide between two or more possibilities. *opportunity* or *power* to *decide*. This is an awesome responsibility and speaks to the fact that we always have choices, no matter the circumstance. The choices we make either build or erode trust.

Recognizing the **opportunity, power**, and, more importantly, the **responsibility** of our choices is key to character development.

There are seven (7) values central to understanding the power, opportunity, and responsibility of C.H.O.I.C.E.S.:

    C – Commitment
    H – Honesty
    O – Openness
    I – Initiative
    C – Communication
    E – Engagement
    S – Service

C – Commitment. The act of binding yourself (intellectually or emotionally) to a course of action. – vocabulary.com[xcix]

> Make a commitment to doing what is right, not just what is convenient or easy.

H – Honesty. The quality or condition of being truthful and fair; integrity; steadfast adherence to a strict moral or ethical code. – MerriamWebster.com[c]

> Be honest and forthright in your actions.

O – Openness. Characterized by an attitude of ready accessibility (especially about one's actions or purposes); not secretive; willingness or readiness to receive (especially impressions or ideas). – Vocabulary.com[ci]

> Demonstrate genuine interest and be open to the ideas of others.

I – Initiative. The readiness and willingness to take the first steps in an undertaking; the individual desire to succeed. – seslisozluk.net [cii]

> Be ready to engage in positive action.

C – Communication. The transmission of information so that the recipient understands what the sender intends; the process of exchanging information and ideas. An active process, it involves encoding, transmitting, and decoding intended messages. – CBV.ns[ciii]

> Effective communication is necessary to understand and to be understood.

E – Engagement. The act of sharing in the activities of a group; emotional involvement or commitment. – Freedictionary.com[civ]

> Stay present, focused, and connected when interacting with others.

S – Service. Work done by one person or group that benefits another. – Xuhua Chen.[cv] Excellent customer service is "…the process by which your organization delivers its services or products in a way that allows the customer to access them in the most efficient, fair, cost effective, and humanly satisfying and pleasurable manner possible." - Jack Speer

> Service is a core value of leadership.

Leaders must recognize the opportunity, power, and responsibility of their C.H.O.I.C.E.S. and never sacrifice integrity or character for 15 minutes of fame.

C.H.O.I.C.E.S.

Commitment, Honesty, Openness, Initiative, Communication, Engagement, Service

We all make choices and we are responsible for the choices we make.

Albert Schweitzer:

Success is not the key to happiness. Happiness is the key to success. If you love what you are doing, you will be successful.

Helen Keller:

I long to accomplish a great and noble task, but it is my chief duty to accomplish humble tasks as though they were great and noble. The world is moved along, not only by the mighty shoves of its heroes, but also by the aggregate of the tiny pushes of each honest worker.

Unknown:

Excellence is never an accident; it is always the result of high intention, sincere effort, intelligent direction, skillful execution and the vision to see obstacles as opportunities.

Commitment – The act of binding yourself (intellectually or emotionally) to a course of action. – vocabulary.com

Honesty – The quality or condition of being honest; integrity; steadfast adherence to a strict moral or ethical code. – Merriam Webster

Openness – Characterized by an attitude of ready accessibility (especially about one's actions or purposes); not secretive; willingness or readiness to receive (especially impressions or ideas). – vocabulary.com

Initiative – The readiness and willingness to take the first steps in an undertaking; the individual desire to succeed. – seslisozluk.net

Communication – The transmission of information so that the recipient understands what the sender intends; the process of exchanging information and ideas. An active process, it involves encoding, transmitting, and decoding intended messages. – CBV.ns

Engagement – The act of sharing in the activities of a group; emotional involvement or commitment. – Freedictionary.com

Service - Work done by one person or group that benefits another. – Xuhua Chen. Excellent customer service is "…the process by which your organization delivers its services or products in a way that allows the customer to access them in the most efficient, fair, cost effective, and humanly satisfying and pleasurable manner possible." – Jack Speer

Anonymous:

One evening an old Cherokee told his grandson about a battle that goes on inside people. He said,

"My son, the battle is between two wolves inside us all.

One is Evil. It is anger, envy, jealousy, sorrow, regret, greed, arrogance, self-pity, guilt, resentment, inferiority, lies, false pride, superiority, and ego.

The other is Good. It is joy, peace, love, hope, serenity, humility, kindness, benevolence, empathy, generosity, truth, compassion and faith."

The grandson thought about it for a minute and then asked his grandfather,

"Which wolf wins?"

The old Cherokee simply replied,

"The one you feed."

> Commitment is what transforms a promise into reality.
> – Abraham Lincoln

Leaders Demonstrate Commitment

I served as a groomsman in the wedding of a good friend. During the ceremony, the minister made a comment to the newlyweds that was appropriate for everyone involved in a committed relationship.

> In life, there will always be ups and downs, but if you can remember the feelings you have at this very moment in time, the optimism, love, commitment, caring, possibilities that you are feeling right now, then you can weather the storms.

I have heard the words "ups and downs" and "weathering storms" at many wedding ceremonies, but the added charge to "remember the feelings you have at this very moment in time; optimism, love, commitment, caring, and possibilities," added something special. It was great advice! Later, at the reception, the father of the bride made a toast to the newlyweds:

> The key to a successful marriage is to continue to fall in love with one another over and over again. To always remember what you enjoy about this person and commit to that feeling over and over again.

It would be great if we could apply these ideals to all the *committed* relationships we have, both personal and professional. I know it can sound strange to say, *fall in love over and over again* with personal and professional relationships, but think about the reasons you decided to commit to anything or anyone you considered important.

Many of us in committed relationships are seasoned and cynical and can rip apart the statements of the minister and the father of the bride with ease. We can find fault in their philosophy, call them naïve or overly simplistic. We can refute and complicate their statements with the statistical fact that in the US 40%–50% of marriages end in divorce or permanent separation.[cvi] But, those *facts* do not render the toast useless nor do they make the words of the minister null and void.

Any *meaningful* relationship requires dedication and hard work to make it successful. We engage in committed relationships with a different level of passion, purpose, thought, trust, dedication, and love; that is why they are called *committed*.

I remember the words my father said when he presided over my wedding:

> Today's ceremony is only a legal formality. You already made the real commitment to one another when you said 'Yes' and were engaged months earlier. Every relationship has a beginning where you make choices about character, shared values, beliefs, and ideals that bring you closer together. You look at the good and the bad and weigh the possibilities of 'If' you could be together. By the time you get to the point of a wedding, you should have learned the core values of the other person. - Rev. Robert Lee Davis, Sr.

Commitment implies engagement; talking, listening, experiencing the ups and the downs, working through problems, seeing one another at their best and their worst, and deciding with both eyes open that this is the right choice.

The commitment you make is strengthened as you let down barriers and allow your partner inside to the *real* you; the *you* that is confident *and* unsure, decisive *and* confused, stable *and* moody, well-groomed *and* disheveled. When you can see these truths and still move closer together, you will have the ability to fall in love over and over again.

All commitments take a leap of faith, and yes, even with all the effort in the world, things may not work out. But, maintaining perspective, committing to the fact that life has ups and downs, remembering the feelings of optimism, <u>and</u> being able to fall in love repeatedly with everything important that you do, makes that leap of faith easier.

There is no such thing as an unimportant or insignificant relationship. – Dr. Larry Roper

Leaders Recognize The Importance Of Developing Relationships

I was co-facilitating a workshop sponsored by Dr. Larry Roper, the Vice Provost for Student Affairs at Oregon State University. At the close of the workshop Larry used a phrase that I had never heard before, "Manage each other's reputation." It referred to the responsibility and consequences of our conversations.

Many of us have experience with someone *mis*-managing our reputation with rumors, gossip, misinformation, and public discussion of private information. Managing each other's reputation is an excellent way for leaders to demonstrate their commitment to one another as professionals.

Larry's words left a lasting impression, and I was pleased that he published his ideas in an article titled, On Being a Professional.

> Every conversation that we have about another person we are either positively managing or mismanaging their reputation. In committed relationships colleagues take responsibility for managing the reputations of others. This requires that we monitor ourselves and interrupt situations where others try to draw us into conversations that do not treat others well. In the process of managing other's reputations we are also managing our own.[cvii]

Larry believes that the foundation of professionalism is relationship building.

> There is no such thing as an unimportant or insignificant relationship. Every person and every interaction matters... Each human interaction that we have, in some way, influences how we feel about ourselves, how we are perceived, the success that we achieve, and the legacy that we will leave...[cviii]

If we truly believe that "there is no such thing as an unimportant or insignificant relationship," then we will act appropriately to care for one another. Larry shares nine (9) communication and engagement principles which, if adhered to, can create more open, engaging, and respectful communities.

1. Do not start the conversation unless you are committed to the other person.
2. Listen generously.
3. Be on each other's side.
4. Speak your truth.
5. Take care of the other person.
6. Stay focused in the conversation and stay in the conversation until it is complete.
7. Treat the conversation and each person as if they matter.
8. Be clear about the value that you are producing.
9. Manage each other's reputation.[cix]

How do we translate these ideas into *positive* actions? Being aware of our actions is the first step and making a conscious effort to change behaviors that undermine relationships is the second.

Relationship building is a critical component of leadership and requires individuals to take personal responsibility for their actions, see no relationship as unimportant or insignificant, and treat people with dignity.

All relationships take time and effort to develop and maintain, but we sometime fail in relationship building because of the distractions around us, especially at work.

> The quality of our relationships with others has a powerful impact on our ability to progress and get things done in our institutions. However, because of our focus on task accomplishment we often do not give complete consideration to showing care for relationships. The busyness of our personal and work lives can lead to sloppiness in attending to the needs of others. The challenge before student affairs professionals [*or any professional for that matter*] is to develop an approach that places relationships with others at the center of both our personal and professional life. Being thoughtful about the quality of our relationships and showing generosity in our dealings with others are essential components of being effective in life and work.[cx]

If we care about one another, then we will work to become fully aware of how we engage with others, including controlling what we say. This is the essence of managing one another's reputation and can help strengthen personal and professional relationships.

I have learned over the years that when one's mind is made up, this diminishes fear; knowing what must be done does away with fear. – Rosa Parks

Leaders Do Not Fear Change

During the month of June in 2015, the United States experienced extraordinary events impacting traditions and policies many believed were inviolable or unalterable. They included the removal of Confederate flags and monuments from state capitals across the South, upholding the core tenants of the Affordable Care Act, and legalizing same-sex marriage nationwide.

There are strong feelings about these decisions, but taking a moment to think as well as feel can be helpful in developing a more productive perspective on the changes impacting our nation and the world.

On June 17, 2015, nine African American parishioners were murdered during a prayer service at the Mother Emanuel African Methodist Episcopal Church in Charleston, South Carolina by a white supremacist intent on starting a race war. This was a heartbreaking and senseless tragedy, but it resulted in the removal of the Confederate flag from the South Carolina State House grounds and served as a catalyst for the removal of Confederate battle flags and civil war monuments from public lands and private institutions across the South. The result of this appalling act was to unify a community not divide it. In his July 2, 2015 Op-Ed responding to a recent unity march, South Carolina State Senator Chip Campsen wrote, "Sunday night the Charleston community demonstrated an outpouring of unity when over 15,000 held hands across the Ravenel Bridge…Let us follow the examples set before us. If the Confederate flag on our statehouse grounds upsets a significant number of citizens, let's remove it in the name of peace and mutual upbuilding."[cxi]

On June 25, 2015, the King v. Burwell decision by the Supreme Court safeguarded the core tenants of the Patient Protection and Affordable Care Act (ACA). Chief Justice Roberts stated that "Congress passed the Affordable Care Act to improve health insurance markets, not to destroy them. If at all possible we must interpret the Act in a way that is consistent with the former, and avoids the latter."[cxii]

On June 26, 2015, the Supreme Court ruled in Obergefell v. Hodges, finding "…that the fundamental right to marry is guaranteed to same-sex couples by both the Due Process Clause and the Equal Protection Clause of the Fourteenth Amendment to the United States Constitution. The 5–4 ruling requires all fifty states to perform and recognize the marriages of same-sex couples on the same terms and conditions as the marriages of opposite-sex couples, with all the accompanying rights and responsibilities."[cxiii]

We are truly witnessing historic change; change in our understanding of an iconic image and the history it represents, change in the allocation of resources and how we care for our citizens, and change in our national view of the equality of love.

Our personal perspectives and our individual values are inextricably bound to our national identity. With these decisions, there are those who believe their personal values and our national identity are under attack.

There are others who believe that the nation has grown and matured into a more accepting, tolerant, and loving nation, where history is placed in the context of the current impact on the citizenry and not through sanguine memories of a past that was not tolerant, united, or inclusive; where political brinksmanship is ultimately reviewed and settled under the aegis of the law, and where the definition of equality is broad enough to accept a more inclusive definition of love.

How we engage with one another as we discuss the changes impacting our society and our differing perspectives must be done with dignity, respect, and love.

Our perspectives need not be rooted in stone, making us inflexible, intolerant, or unwilling to see the opportunities that come with change. We must not let our misunderstanding of the *other* lock us into the belief that *change* itself is bad.

A change of perspective can be transformative, opening new possibilities of seeing, doing, and being. The difficult part of change is allowing ourselves to see events in a different light – especially when we are so wrapped up in our routines, beliefs, and desired outcomes.

These entrenched routines and beliefs can stifle our growth and limit our ability to truly connect across lines of difference. We stifle ourselves personally and professionally because we instinctively hold on to what we *know*, relying on the canons, "that's how it's always been done," "that's what I've always been taught," etc.

A change of perspective involves looking inward, taking an honest assessment of how we act, how we feel, what we say our values are, and how we demonstrate those values.

This is what leaders do. We recognize that self-examination is necessary for growth. It allows us to make better decisions - not based solely on what we have heard, how we were raised, or what we accepted without question - but based on a critical examination of our beliefs coupled with facts.

Potentially, this self-examination and decision-making forces us to look at ourselves, our beliefs, our actions, and our times in a different light. This search for understanding (SCD), can ultimately lead to peace of mind and a connection to a larger more inclusive community.

Leaders do not fear change.
They lead and mange through times of change.

As we look to form a more perfect union, examine your beliefs, stay engaged with the conversations, and do not fear change.

Stop letting people who do so little for you control so much of your mind, feelings and emotions. – Will Smith

Leaders Control The First Move And Intend To Engage Meaningfully

In martial arts, the first rule of engaging an opponent is to control the first move. For those new to the practice or unaware of the principle, controlling the first move is simply preparing yourself, your mind and body, to be present in the moment.

Controlling the first move is not about your opponent's style or skill, being fast, striking first, or practicing the moves in your head – all those thoughts can be distractions – it is about allowing your mind and body to be focused so that you can engage appropriately.

> Flow with whatever may happen, and let your mind be free: Stay centered by accepting whatever you are doing. This is the ultimate. – Zhuangzi, Nan-Hua-Ch'en-Ching, or, the Treatise of the transcendent master from Nan-Hua

> Controlling the first move is to have control of yourself.

Having a mind and body at peace, which leads to clarity of purpose, is difficult to achieve. It is a life-long process that requires continuous training, repetition, and reflection.

> Train tirelessly to defeat the greatest enemy, yourself, and to discover the greatest master, yourself. – Shi Su Yan

> We all have inner demons to fight. We call these demons 'fear,' and 'hatred,' and 'anger.' If you don't conquer them, then a life of a hundred years is a tragedy. If you do, a life of a single day can be a triumph. – Yip Man

Miyamoto Musashi, the renowned swordsman and author of <u>The Book of Five Rings</u>, stated, "The true science of martial arts means practicing them in such a way that they will be useful at any time, and to teach them in such a way that they will be useful in all things."

Although we may not be engaging in physical combat, our mind can be a swirling maelstrom of emotions that needs to be conquered. At work, we can be so task-focused and metric-driven that we enter into engagements with negative anticipation, annoyance, and impatience. In our personal lives, we can be so distracted by news, bills, politics, and the fad of the day, that we avoid engagements and spend little time nurturing relationships or paying attention to what really matters.

These distractions act as debris that impede our ability to be optimistic about our circumstances, see the positive potential in others, or be at peace and present in the moment. Clearing our mind of the debris of negative anticipation opens the way for our personal and professional engagements to be more fulfilling.

Everyone must find their own path to controlling the first move, but whatever choice you make must include continuous training, repetition, and reflection. An effective support tool on your journey is the mindset of I.T.E.M.

Intend **T**o **E**ngage **M**eaningfully

I.T.E.M. is a mantra that allows for purposeful thoughts and behaviors when engaging with others and changes the mindset from one of negative anticipation to one of positive intent.

When we are intentional in how we interact with others, we control the first move through purposeful engagement and act with a belief that people, and relationships are important.

Controlling the first move and practicing the mantra of I.T.E.M. prepares the mind and body to be present in the moment and creates *positive* self-fulfilling prophecies. Finding inner peace by controlling one's self contributes to positive personal and professional relationships and is a goal worth fighting for no matter how difficult the journey.

Alone we can do so little; together we can do so much.
– Helen Keller

Leaders Recognize The Value Of Team

The pinnacle of competition in the sports world are the Olympic Games. They provide an opportunity to compete against the best athletes in the world, witness individual excellence, and watch in awe at the record shattering victories. We also witness the tremendous importance of teamwork.

Team sports provide an opportunity to experience the synergy created by working together in support of a common goal and sends a powerful message on the importance of cooperation.

> "Alone we can do so little; together we can do so much."

Helen Keller's quote speaks to the true nature of team and teamwork – not as a theory – but as a practice.

The Oxford Dictionary defines teamwork as:

> The combined action of a group of people, especially when effective and efficient.[cxiv]

The Business Dictionary defines teamwork as:

> The process of working collaboratively with a group of people in order to achieve a goal.[cxv]

These definitions are accurate but omit two critical pieces to move teamwork from theory to practice – synergy and accountability.

Synergy is an interaction or state of being where two or more people, elements, substances, agents, etc., work together in a manner that produces something greater than could be created by individual effort.

With respect to teamwork, synergy requires each person to know their role and act in a manner necessary for the best outcome in the situation. This is called accountability, "A personal choice to rise above one's circumstances and demonstrate the ownership necessary for achieving Key Results; to See It,® Own It,® Solve It,® and Do It.®"[cxvi]

This definition from The Oz Principle embodies the essence of teamwork, as it requires one to think about and act on what is best for the situation at hand, not just follow the program, script, playbook, or procedure that has always been used.

True teamwork is about understanding, execution, and trust.

- Understanding your role.
- Understanding and trusting your team members to know their role(s).
- Understanding how to execute the appropriate behavior in the moment.

Many definitions of teamwork focus on task completion – performing a function for a specific end – and leave out the critical components of synergy and accountability. These two ideals focus on engagement, understanding, trust, knowledge of process, and a desire to do what is best and necessary for the team's success. The team members work together in an accountable and engaged manner to create the best outcome.

When we think about teams and teamwork, we often look outside of the workplace and into the world of sports. No matter what team sports you follow, each player has a specific role: the forward, coxswain, midfielder, back, goalie, libero, quarterback, right winger, offensive striker, etc., all have different responsibilities, but they are all part of the same team. Their cohesion, preparation, and skill determine success or failure. The result of their coordinated efforts is a goal, a score, a record-breaking relay, and hopefully a win.

The result of a well-organized effort in the workplace can often go unnoticed because it is part of our daily routine. When we are solely focused on the "big" sale, the "big" presentation, the "big" client, etc., we often forget about the preparation, research, and people doing the daily tasks – the small victories – that allow the "big" goals to be achieved.

In sports, the great pass, the fast relay, the steals, the tackles, the defensive stops, etc., all contribute to the win. The "assist" is critical to the goal. Good teams recognize, acknowledge, and celebrate their successes together. They also analyze their failures together. They *learn* together.

In most organizations, it is not one department or one superstar who makes it all work; the IT wiz and the brilliant entrepreneur still need the accountants, the receptionist, and the payroll coordinator. Thinkers need doers, dreamers need implementation specialist. We all need people we can rely on.

Let us broaden our idea of teamwork to include the consistent role players as well as the superstars. Let us look at the assist <u>and</u> the goal. As you achieve success do what the athletes do; slide across the field, embrace one another and do your victory dance. Just remember the concerted effort it took from the *entire* team to help reach the goal.

It's kind of fun to do the impossible. – Walt Disney

Leaders Have Fun

Many companies are searching for the holy grail of programs, tools, or ideas to drive employee engagement and productivity. Although there is no panacea program that will meet every company's needs, consider the SPF system when deciding on an engagement strategy.

SPF = Simplicity, Positivity, and Fun.

<u>Simplicity</u> – Grow great ideas by providing opportunities for engagement.
<u>Positivity</u> – Focus on what can be done better, not just on what is being done wrong.
<u>Fun</u> – Make participation fun, easy, and rewarding. Provide rewards and incentives as well as opportunities to recognize and celebrate great ideas.

Using the SPF System can be an effective strategy to support or enhance any engagement program.

I am often asked if implementing a suggestion box is a good way to foster employee engagement. While it is always best to support open and direct communication between employees and employers, in the absence of other programs the suggestion box can be an effective option. If it does not turn into the anonymous complaint box, and the employer reviews, acknowledges, and implements the good ideas, it can be a great tool.

Some organizations have very structured systems for employee engagement. William L. McKnight, a former President and CEO at 3M is credited with telling his managers to, "Encourage experimental doodling," and created the "15 percent rule." This policy encourages risk taking and allows employees to use 15% of their paid time to work on their most passionate ideas. Hewlett-Packard implemented the "management by walking around" (MBWA) process, as a tool to connect senior leaders with the people working on the front lines.

> ... In MBWA practice, managers spend a significant amount of their time making informal visits to work area and listening to the employees. The purpose of this exercise is to collect qualitative information, listen to

suggestions and complaints, and keep a finger on the pulse of the organization. Also called management by wandering around.[cxvii]

If the purpose is clear, and staff and management are successfully engaging with one another, implement what works.

Although there are many great employee engagement models out there, some organizations still want to provide a simple and anonymous vehicle for employees to share ideas. This brings us back to the suggestion box.

If you want to use this approach, here are a few pointers:

<u>Share your vision</u> – Meet with your leadership teams and employees to discuss the purpose, process, and desired outcomes of using a suggestion or ideas box. Share the organizational vision so that everyone understands the rationale and the intent of the process. Make sure to differentiate between facility requests, unreasonable requests or complaints, and the types of ideas that can potentially help the company grow.

<u>Read every suggestion</u> – You never know when you might find the diamond in the rough, or a seed for a new innovative product, service, or process.

<u>Share the ideas with the organization</u> – As often as is practical, share the good, the bad, and the ugly ideas with the organization. Acknowledge the suggestions you can use and offer feedback on the ideas that are inappropriate or not practical for the organization.

<u>Reward the ideas that help the company</u> – Always acknowledge and reward success. Even if the suggestion was anonymous, it is important to make a big deal of the ideas that helped the organization grow or meet a departmental need.

<u>Do not create a complicated process</u> – The environment you create matters. Forcing people to provide ideas or suggestions is different from providing opportunities to share. Whether it is in meetings, through on-line resources, or through a traditional box in the employee lounge, engaging with employees to help drive the success of the organization is what matters.

Ideally the suggestions will help the company excel in customer service, improve communication with employees and external clients, and encourage and recognize innovation. Just be prepared to read the occasional comments about the quality of the food in the vending machines, the number of years without a raise, or the lack of quality toilet paper in the bathrooms.

Do not let these occasional comments get you down; remember, reading every suggestion will make you more aware of employee concerns and potentially allow you to address real morale issues.

Work with your teams, engage, listen, and succeed. Put those employee engagement ideas into practice and apply plenty of SPF.

It is not enough to understand, or to see clearly. The future will be shaped in the arena of human activity, by those willing to commit their minds and their bodies to the task. – Robert Kennedy

Leaders Do Not Need A Crystal Ball To Predict The Future

The beginning of the year is always full of predictions for business. Workshops, articles, and business reports discuss trends and pitfalls for the upcoming year. While the articles are interesting, they may not provide new information on the progressive actions businesses should engage in to maintain organizational and employee success. There is a focus on external resources – tools, processes, programs, etc. – to help spur success, but not much focus on the untapped creativity and expertise within organizations.

I have seen many owners look outside of their organizations instead of looking in; they adopt business practices that do not pertain to their industry, ignore good information because they do not like the messenger, and adopt quick fixes because the longer-term fix seems too hard to implement or will not generate an immediate ROI. They completely ignore the insights of the people doing the actual work, so they might as well be looking at a crystal ball for answers and wishing for the best.

Progressive businesses use appropriate metrics, trends, and goal setting strategies to plan for their future; they also share the organizational goals with the entire team and solicit feedback.

- They fold the organizational expectations into their daily actions,
- share information company-wide, and
- expect all staff members (not just managers or supervisors) to pay attention to business opportunities, industry trends, technology, etc., that can help the organization grow.

Progressive businesses foster an environment where everyone has a voice and is encouraged to share ideas that can help the company maintain a competitive edge.

I have met many chief executives who do not agree with this idea. They believe that if you give employees a voice and let them express ideas for business growth or organizational direction, there will be too many people *sharing ideas* and not enough people being productive.

Good leaders and organizations with strong cultures listen to their staff members, gather information without the fear of thinking their employees are taking over, and know that not every idea brought forward must be implemented.

A CEO shared with me that he had a practice of not acknowledging ideas, because "Employees would expect to be listened to all the time and might share stupid ideas." I had another COO share their belief that if they solicited ideas from their team members, they were obligated to use them. So, they did not solicit ideas.

I am not advocating for companies to be completely democratic or implement all ideas, that is a recipe for disaster. I am suggesting that progressive leaders should engage their employees in conversations, solicit input on ideas, and provide opportunities for their teams to help the company succeed.

Correcting the misconception that all ideas brought forward will be implemented is a function of effective communication. Just be clear about the process and thank people for their input, suggestions, and ideas. Let staff know that you will take their feedback seriously and figure out what works best for the organization.

I believe that providing a vehicle for open communication is vitally important for the success of any organization. The knowledge and wisdom of your staff members could be the key to unlocking infinite possibilities. Information is power, but only if you have the information and know what to do with it. Good organizations keep their ears open and encourage their staff members to share thoughts, insights, and ideas.

Encourage employee engagement through an exercise called "If I Ran The Company." This program challenges employees to present ideas individually and in teams on the specific programs, projects, and practices they think will help the organization succeed.

Employees brainstorm ideas, look at interdepartmental deficiencies, poor processes, organizational silos, etc., and set out to find the best <u>internal</u> resources (people, departments, systems, etc.,) to help make their ideas a reality.

This exercise challenges participants to go one step further than just presenting an idea; it tasks them to figure out how to pay for their ideas. Participants share the resources needed, projected costs and benefits, and the timeframe needed to bring the product or process to life. This exercise asks staff to think like owners.

Engaging your staff and encouraging them to "Run the Company" means that you provide them with information, opportunities, and resources to understand why the ideas could be great, or not so great, for the company. Trust your teams to think about the success of the organization.

The "If I Ran The Company" exercise was designed to solicit ideas, but also to bring individuals, groups, and departments together to think about the success of the organization on more than a cursory or selfish level. It produces actionable ideas, encourages teamwork, and exposes weaknesses in processes. It can also identify potential leaders, individuals who can think about the broader implications of their ideas.

Anyone can have a moment where they complain about another department, process, or product and say, "If I ran the company, I would do something different." But our experience shows that very few people spend time and effort understanding the real impact their ideas would have on the organization.

When leaders challenge their staff teams to find ways to strengthen the organization and give them the time and tools to understand the potential impact of their ideas, they can create a stronger more engaged workforce.

You hired your employees to do more than just complete tasks – your hired them to make your organization excellent. Give them every tool to run the company and you will not need a crystal ball to know that your future will be bright.

Too many problem-solving sessions become battlegrounds where decisions are made based on power rather than intelligence. – Margaret J. Wheatley

Leaders Actively Engage In Problem Solving

What are you willing to do to help solve problems?

The answer to that question may determine how successful any leader, company, or team will be. We each play a role in influencing the organizations we work for. Our attitudes and actions have a specific and direct impact on the work environment.

All organizations benefit from engaged and committed employees. If you are one who sees problems with people, process, execution, etc., but <u>only</u> offer criticism without solutions, then you are part of the problem.

Don't find fault, find a remedy. – Henry Ford

Always be willing to help. We are all responsible for our behaviors. We <u>choose</u> if we will positively engage with others even when we are tired, frustrated, bored, distracted, etc. This is especially true in the workplace. It takes effort and commitment to do a job, so why work for a company if you dislike the people and the work, think you are at the worst place ever, or believe that nothing will change for the better?

The reason you stay with any organization must be about more than just a paycheck. Even in moments of frustration and anger, if you still have hope then there is the possibility for positive change.

Leaders look for opportunities to make change for the better.

If you throw your hands up in frustration and disengage, you fail yourself and the company you <u>chose</u> to work for. Why not put effort into making the workplace what you need? If you say, "I've tried, and nothing has changed," then there is one question you should ask:

"Have I exhausted every avenue to make positive change in my organization?"

If the answer is "No," then keep trying. If the answer is "Yes," then ask yourself:

"Do I care anymore?"

If the answer is "No," then you should do what is right for you and the company and find another profession or organization that makes you happy. If you are frustrated and have no hope for positive change then your actions will be a roadblock to others who believe that change is possible.

Organizations are like living organisms, they function best when all the parts are working together well. An organization cannot truly be successful if the people, departments, units, etc., are in constant conflict.

The people who make up the organization must work together to fix problems. They need to be persistent and solution-driven with a mindset for collaboration.

All companies have imperfections, but if employers and employees work together in a concerted manner to solve problems, they can overcome the imperfections and become the best.

Problem solving is a function of leadership. Those with the courage and conviction to work with others to solve problems ultimately succeed.

Nothing in life is to be feared, it is only to be understood. Now is the time to understand more, so that we may fear less. – Marie Curie

Leaders Move From "Why Me?" To "Now What?"

At some point, all leaders ask the question "Why me?" The question is often asked when one is dealing with difficult situations as part of a search for answers.

Asking "Why me?" can be useful if we are able to rationally analyze the incident(s) and find reasonable and/or actionable answers. It can also pull us down into despair and guilt if we do not find the answers we need. For situations that are out of our control there may be no meaningful answers, and the question, "Why me?" may never be resolved. But for those difficult situations that are in our control, the follow-up question for committed leaders should be, "Now what?"

The phrase "Why me?" is passive and can demonstrate a lack of ownership, responsibility, or control of the next steps. The phrase "Now what?" can be a catalyst for positive change, as it is action-oriented and should help us take the appropriate steps to move forward, regain control, and avoid repeating mistakes. If your "Now what?" question is not a retreat into more self-doubt, frustration, and despair, it can be used as a powerful statement that allows you to think clearly, acknowledge mistakes, and prepare for positive resolution.

Mistakes are lessons that can help us make better decisions in the future – if we learn from them. Doing the same things repeatedly and expecting different results keeps us mired in the "Why me?" malaise. For example:

- If we talk about customer service but we do not treat customers well, then we cannot say, "Why me?' when we lose clients.
- If we do not follow through on our assignments, then we cannot say "Why me?" when tasks are taken away and we receive poor performance reviews.
- If we mismanage our colleagues' reputations, then we cannot say "Why me?" when we have a lack of harmony.
- If we are not open to new ideas, then we cannot say "Why me?" when innovation stops.

We all make mistakes - we drop the ball in our personal and professional lives - that is the nature of being human. If our actions truly are *mistakes* and not consistent or intentional patterns of behavior, we may be able to repair any damage we have caused.

A "Now what?" attitude requires accepting responsibility for our actions and then asking common-sense questions that move us toward positive action. Questions like:

- What happened?
- Why did it happen, and how can I ensure that the situation does not happen again?
- Where can I find the best ideas to resolve the issues?
- What follow-up is necessary?
- Who do I need to inform?
- Who can I ask for help?

Adopting a "Now what?" attitude can be one of the more positive steps a leader can take to achieve their mission, vision, and goals.

By acknowledging our mistakes, avoiding debilitating guilt, and letting our follow-up actions prove our true intentions, we can move from "Why me?" to "Now what?" and face the biggest challenges with optimism and courage.

Just one step. Just one mile. Just one dollar. Just one kiss. Just one person. When we look at life through the lens of 'one,' everything becomes that much more attainable. – Mick Ebeling

Leaders Know The Magic Number

> …changing the world can happen anywhere and anyone can do it…. but the question is — what will the world look like after you change it? - Admiral William H. McRaven

There was one week in 2015 that had the most compelling numbers:

- 800 million
- 400 million
- 38 million
- 21,372
- 101
- 1

$800 million – The box office receipts for Avengers: Age of Ultron. This sequel scored the second biggest box-office opening with $187.7 million, and grossed close to $800 million worldwide since its release on Friday, May 1, 2015. – thenumbers.com and LA Times[cxviii]

$400 million+ – The take-home pay for the Mayweather vs. Pacquiao fight. Mayweather made $250 million to $275 million, with Pacquiao clearing $170 million to $190 million.[cxix]

38 million – The number of people displaced within their own country by conflict or violence. "A record-breaking 38 million people have been displaced within their own country by conflict or violence. This is the equivalent of the total populations of London, New York and Beijing combined. 'These are the worst figures for forced displacement in a generation, signaling our complete failure to protect innocent civilians,' said Jan Egeland, secretary general at the Norwegian Refugee Council (NRC)."[cxx]

21,372 – The injured and death toll from the devastating magnitude 7.8 earthquake that struck Nepal in April 2015. As the rescue and clean-up efforts continued, the National Emergency Operation Center recorded 7,250 fatalities and 14,122 injuries.[cxxi]

101 – The age of the oldest survivor to be pulled from under the rubble in Nepal.[cxxii]

1 – The number of people it takes to make a difference.

Sometimes our priorities seem out of whack with the greater societal needs. The $800 million in ticket sales or the more than $400 million in payouts from the "big fight" could go a long way in helping the 38 million displaced people and those suffering from natural disasters.

Whatever your thoughts and feelings about the numbers, what is true is that individual actions can have a profound impact on the world. The influence of an actor, director, or writer can fill the seats and inspire people to wait in line for hours to see the final product. The reputation of two boxers can create a Pay-For-View frenzy. The actions of a dictator or a warlord can have incredible consequences for millions of people, creating suffering, chaos, and fear.

Each one of us is connected to one of these numbers in some way – whether we watched the movie, watched the fight, know someone who is displaced because of war or tyranny, have been personally touched by disaster, or inspired by a tale of survival – each one of us is impacted by the actions of another, which leads to the last number – 1.

Each one of us has an impact on another person. Our individual actions can have a ripple effect that impacts the world. We have a choice in whether that impact is positive or negative.

At the 2014 commencement speech at the University of Texas at Austin, Naval Admiral William H. McRaven spoke about the power of "1" and the 800 million-to-1 ratio:

> Tonight, there are almost 8,000 students graduating from UT. That great paragon of analytical rigor. Ask.Com, says that the average American will meet 10,000 people in their lifetime. That's a lot of folks. But, if every one of you changed the lives of just 10 people — and each one of those folks changed the lives of another 10 people — just 10 — then in five generations — 125 years — the class of 2014 will have changed the lives of 800 million people.[cxxiii]

For many, thinking about changing the world seems to be an impossible or unreasonable goal. One might ask, "In a world of billions, how can '1' make a difference?"

To harness the power of "1" to impact the world, follow these steps:

- Start each day with a task completed.
- Find someone to help you through life.
- Respect everyone.
- Know that life is not fair and that you will fail often.
- But if you take some risks, step up when the times are toughest, face down the bullies, lift up the downtrodden and never, ever give up — if you do these things, then the next generation and the generations that follow will live in a world far better than the one we have today.[cxxiv]

We must remember that we are inextricably connected to one another. Therefore, every "1" matters.

> If I have learned anything in my time traveling the world, it is the power of hope. The power of one person — Washington, Lincoln, King, Mandela and even a young girl from Pakistan, Malala — one person can change the world by giving people hope.[cxxv]

"1" person can have a tremendous impact on the world.

That "1" person is you.

> Let us remember: One book, one pen, one child, and one teacher can change the world. – Malala Yousafzai

Peace is not the absence of conflict but the presence of creative alternatives for responding to conflict - alternatives to passive or aggressive responses, alternatives to violence. – Dorothy Thompson

Leaders Resolve Conflict

Benjamin Franklin is credited with the statement, "In this world nothing can be said to be certain, except death and taxes." But even more certain is that, "In life there will be conflict." Unfortunately, leaders do not always know how to appropriately address conflict, often choosing to avoid rather than confront problems.

What is conflict?

> Conflict is a form of competitive behavior between people or groups. It occurs when two or more people compete over perceived or actual incompatible goals or limited resources. (Bouldering, 1962). Conflict, however, is different from the kinds of competition that occur in games. In games, people cooperate and compete to have fun. In conflict, people may have physical or psychological harm as their goal.[cxxvi]

Author Wayne Dyer states that "Conflict cannot survive without your participation." More importantly it cannot be resolved without your participation.

Unresolved conflict is one of the top reasons productivity suffers in the workplace. Unresolved conflict can destroy a work community just as easily as it can destroy personal relationships.

In the article The Hidden Costs of Workplace Conflict, Steve McGuire explains:

> Conflict is an inevitable aspect of any organization's existence. As Dr. Dan Dana of the Dana Mediation Institute points out, workplace conflict follows a predictable, retaliatory path when two or more task interdependent employees find fault with the other and utilize perceptions and behaviors that end up causing a business problem. Dana estimates that "65% of all employee performance problems are due to bad *relationships*, not bad employees…"[cxxvii] - Steve McGuire

It is important that leaders recognize what conflict looks like, how it manifests, and address the conflict early. The key to resolution is understanding the causes and symptoms of conflict.

In their white paper How Much Is Conflict Costing You, John Ford and Associates explain conflict this way:

> …Conflict is a difference about how expected needs are going to be met and we typically know we are in a conflict because of the emotional tension we experience. At a behavioral level, we become aware of either distancing or combative strategies: gossip, avoidance, verbal abuse, passive/aggressive communication, and hostility. Conflict can be demonstrated by not returning phone calls, not having coffee with your colleague anymore and filing complaints, grievances or lawsuits. At its combative extreme, conflict involves physical violence.[cxxviii]

Unresolved conflict can keep coworkers from communicating effectively, result in missing information critical to task completion, professional, and personal development, and disrupt the effective administration of business. Conflict in the workplace also has a financial cost.

> The cost of resolving a conflict can involve the salaries of as many as four employees: the two who are in conflict, their manager, and the HR manager. It is estimated that Fortune 500 senior HR executives spend up to 20% of their time in litigation activities. Studies show that up to 30% of a typical manager's time is spent dealing with conflict.[cxxix]

If colleagues, the people who should be working towards the same goals, cannot effectively confront one another, how can organizations reach their true potential?

Successful organizations have products and/or services that drive growth and support stability. Regardless of the product created, success is ultimately determined by the relationships between individuals and teams and by their ability to communicate effectively and act responsibly in support of the mission, vision, values, and goals. Unresolved conflict inevitably impedes success.

The most common reason for avoiding conflict is not knowing how to confront someone appropriately. There are those who believe that *conflict* is the same as *combat*, and they want to avoid a fight. Conflict refers to friction, disagreement, or discord. Combat refers to a fight or a battle.

> Conflict is a normal part of human engagement.
> Combat is a choice in how we respond to conflict.

We often avoid conflict, hoping that the problem or the person will go away. With regard to addressing conflict effectively, the axiom "time heals all wounds," is flawed. Time can cause some issues to fester, eating away at any possible resolution. The more appropriate saying should be, *Time coupled with deliberate action can possibly heal all wounds.* Without deliberate action, pain, anger, mistrust, etc., between people may not be resolved.

As part of my SCD process, I attended a conference on communication and strengthening relationships; specifically attending sessions on conflict resolution, and learned the following:

1. Anger and unresolved conflict are toxic to any relationship. Whether with a colleague or a life partner, unresolved conflict is a nagging burning fire in our emotional world. Sometimes it is a raging forest fire, other times it is smoldering embers. But if it is not addressed it can consume you.

2. People must forgive one another. Forgiveness is a big word, but it is necessary for resolution. James C. Hunter defines forgiveness as "Giving up resentment when wronged." We often want to hold on to anger, hold on to the words or the actions so that we can keep the other person at bay. But holding on to resentment may hurt you more than the other person. It takes a lot of energy to maintain anger. Ask yourself if all that negative energy could be used for something positive.

3. People in conflict have different views of the same incident. It is vitally important to discuss the conflict and clarify the *intent* of the action vs. the *impact* of the action. The best intentions can have a negative impact when we are unaware of the feelings connected with a set of behaviors. Perception, time, place, mood, etc., all play a role in how we receive information. If a misunderstanding is not addressed, it can spiral out of control because there is an assumption as to the intent from one party and the reality of the impact from another.

The following techniques can be helpful when working through conflict:

- Let the person tell their story. Hear the person out. Let them explain their thoughts and the feelings about the conflict *without interruption*. This shows that you are interested in understanding the reason for the behavior and not solely interested in debate.

- <u>Acknowledge the pain and the offense.</u> Never tell someone how they should feel. Allow someone to experience the pain of the offense in their own unique manner.

- <u>View the offense in consideration of the relationship.</u> Friends, colleagues, family members all have a history. Think about the incident considering the history and the relationship you have with one another. Decide if the incident can be a footnote in your history together or will it end the story. Remember the story is still being written.

- <u>Purpose to forgive.</u> If you *purpose* in your mind or heart to forgive someone, then you will be successful. What is the purpose of confrontation if not to release?

- <u>Control your demeanor.</u> Arrogance, patronizing behavior, unbridled anger, etc., are not effective techniques to resolve conflict. These emotions might demonstrate that you are upset, but they will not help resolve the issues.

- <u>Recognize the importance of time and place.</u> Try to create a time and a place where you can hear one another. Give yourself time to figure out how to address the issues appropriately. Some behaviors or incidents must be addressed immediately but be aware of the *need* to address behaviors vs. the *want* to address behaviors immediately.

- <u>Remember the objective – forgiveness.</u> If your intent is to try and hurt, embarrass, humiliate, or win, then you are not really interested in forgiveness.

- <u>There must be forgiveness *and* reconciliation.</u> Forgiveness means letting go, reconciliation means setting things right. Understand the cost of your past behaviors and resolve to <u>not</u> make the same mistakes going forward.

Can all problems be resolved? Maybe not, but that should not keep leaders from trying. Conflict and combat are not the same. Learning to resolve conflict is crucial to successful work communities, successful leadership, and a successful life.

People ask the difference between a leader and a boss. The leader leads, and the boss drives. – Theodore Roosevelt

Leaders Recognize The Difference Between Being A "Boss" And Being A "Leader"

Halloween comes once a year, but for many employees, the specter of a scary boss haunts them all year long. Discover how to shed your costume and move from being a boss to becoming a leader.

Working for a bad boss can be one of the *scarier* experiences an employee can have and shapes the way one thinks about work and power. In addition to the high turnover, stress, and poor performance they create, bad bosses can have a debilitating effect on an employee's physical and mental health.

> The psychological climate in which you work has a lot to do with your health and happiness. Recent research has found, perhaps not surprisingly, that bad bosses can affect how your whole family[cxxx] relates to one another. They can also affect your physical health, raising your risk for heart disease.[cxxxi] - The Atlantic.com[cxxxii]

Bad bosses know something is not right; the high turnover, dispirited staff, stressful environment, and poor performance are apparent, but they do not always have the skills to address the root cause of the problems. They find reasons, other than their behaviors, to blame for the toxic environment, often scapegoating their staff and attributing problems to the poor moral and intellectual character or the overall incompetence of their employees. When bosses hold on to these beliefs, they turn the workplace into a veritable house of horrors.

For the bosses who create this type of environment, I have a simple message.

Stop. Being. Evil.

For those who are aware of their style and their impact on others and have no desire to change, you will continue to experience high turnover and a dispirited organization, even if you have financial success.

For those who want to change, you can do it! There is a remedy that does not require a séance. Exercising the negative spirit of the bad boss starts with recognition of the need to change and a desire to become better. A belief in your ability to become a better boss is critical to success. As Henry Ford stated, "Whether you think you can, or you think you can't--you're right."

To effect positive change and leave the monster behind:

> <u>First – recognize that you are not possessed.</u> Your environment, your nature, your location, and your title are not the determinant factors in how you treat others. Take responsibility for your behaviors and think about the positive outcomes you would like to have with your colleagues and employees. Employees are not looking for perfection, but they do want a boss who is competent, honest, genuine, and open to personal and professional growth.
>
> <u>Second – recognize that any process of development or change requires courage.</u> Once you choose to develop your skills or change a behavior, the challenge is to have the courage to stand by your commitment. Having a magic talisman to help you succeed would be great but having a strong will and a steady mantra is more effective.

Joy Moeller, BS, RDH, had a simple and effective mantra, "Practice Makes Permanent." Anything you want to do well requires significant practice. Your focus should be on practicing key positive actions that create permanent positive behaviors. Repetition creates muscle memory and, over time, becomes your natural behavior.

The courage to change and the commitment to be better require the following:

- An awareness of your behavior.

- A desire to change.
- Establishing actionable goals and engaging in consistent action(s) to reach your goals (practice).
- Support on your journey.
- Patience.

Joy never spoke about seeking perfection in her training. She was far too practical and recognized that many people fail on their journey for change because they set a goal of perfection. Instead, she simply stated, "Practice Makes Permanent."

Practice being a better boss and a better person. Focus on excellence and not on perfection.

> Third – stop focusing on power. Power is "The ability or right to control people or things."[cxxxiii] Some bosses believe they not only have the *ability* to control people, but the *right* to control people simply because they have a title. For some, this translates into abusive behavior.

Recognize that with power comes responsibility.

True power in a business sits with every employee who interacts with clients or vendors. Every employee represents the organization and has the power to undermine or support the organization with their actions.

Stop focusing on power. Focus on leadership and responsibility.

Leadership is, "The ability to effectively and responsibly engage with people, processes, and programs, to achieve organizational, team, or individual goals." Management is typically the planning, organizing, directing, and controlling of people and products.

The role of a boss is not to manifest threat or malevolence, but to support the success of the organization by finding the potential in each staff member and helping them do their best to support the organizational mission.

> Fourth – stop being afraid. Fear can be debilitating and can cause anyone, especially bosses, to act in inappropriate ways to hide their fear(s). Whether you have a fear of failure, someone else's knowledge or skill, being wrong, etc., you must combat your fear by working toward a mastery of your profession. Study your craft, work to learn the systems

and processes of your organization, hone your interpersonal skills, and practice employee engagement.

Understanding erodes fear.

Recognize and appreciate your employee's resources; their intelligence, experience, skills, thoughts, opinions, and expertise. Learn from those around you. Continuously strive to understand yourself, your motivations, strengths, and weaknesses, and work to achieve balance. Challenge your negative assumptions about your colleagues and employees and acknowledge the positive qualities and accomplishments of those around you.

Halloween happens once a year, and the scary masks we wear should be put away right after the last trick-or-treater leaves with a bag full of candy. If you have a reputation as an evil boss, you can put that mask away permanently.

Your title as "boss" should hold a greater responsibility to support the organizational goals. Those goals should always include treating people with dignity and respect.

Stop being a scary boss and start being a leader.

If there are flaws they are in ourselves, and our task therefore must be one not of redesign but of renewal and reaffirmation, especially of the standards in which all of us believe. – Elliot Richardson

Leaders Have A Spirit Of Renewal And Happiness

Many leaders look forward to the beginning of the New Year as a time of renewal, promise, and opportunity. They make plans and resolutions and enter the New Year full of enthusiasm and excitement. It is a time for a fresh start.

Renewal, promise, opportunity, happiness, enthusiasm, excitement, and starting fresh… Shouldn't those be feelings we have every day?

Leaders must have a spirit of renewal and happiness all year long, providing guidance, motivation, and support to others along the way. Looking to the New Year as the *only* or most important time for renewal limits the opportunities to inspire, innovate, motivate, and maintain momentum throughout the year.

> Believing in your success should be a continuous resolution.

As you resolve to succeed professionally and personally, keep in mind that success should not come by winning at all costs, or by losing your integrity. Success in business and in life comes from a commitment to building something for others while you are building for yourself.

Successful leaders and successful organizations do not just focus on their own needs, they also extend themselves to others and are genuine in their desire to do "good." Sakyong Mipham, in his book Turning the Mind Into an Ally, explains why this is important:

> When we talk about enlightened society, we aren't talking about some utopia where everyone's enlightened. We're talking about a culture of human beings who know the awakened nature of basic goodness and invoke its energy in order to courageously extend themselves to others. Their motivation is allied with compassion, love, and wisdom. This enlightened attitude is not inhibited: it accommodates and incorporates the vicissitudes of life.[cxxxiv]

> How do we learn from the stainless pure ground of basic goodness? How do we generate a compassionate heart in every encounter? The quickest, most practical way to do this is to keep loosening our grip on ourselves... It all comes back to one of my favorite sayings, "**If you want to be miserable, think about yourself. If you want to be happy, think of others.**" This is how we bring [the] enlightened mind down to earth.[cxxxv]

Think about the implications of "generating a compassionate heart in every encounter or achieving happiness by thinking about others." Whether acting as an organization or an individual, we would have the capacity to listen generously to the needs of clients, colleagues, and friends, and find ways to meet those needs. We would be more engaged in problem solving and focus on lasting solutions not just short-term fixes. We would accept responsibility for our actions, treat others with respect, and always do our best. Imagine what our world would be like if our individual motivations were aligned with compassion, love, and wisdom.

At the start of a New Year, I can think of no greater resolution than having a serving spirit, a mind that considers the needs of others, and a heart open to the best in those around us. These ideals should be renewed daily.

Many of us can demonstrate a serving spirit or consider the needs of others when we are happy, comfortable, and thriving. The real test comes when the going gets tough.

> You may forget how you behaved when the going got tough, but others won't. – Mark Burnett

Ensure that your actions are positive and consistent, maintain your commitment to success by doing what is right, not just what is easy, and hold yourself accountable to living by your values, even in the worst of times.

We will always be remembered by our actions, especially the behaviors we engage in during important or difficult times. Two of the most important characteristics necessary to succeed in difficult times are perspective and perseverance.

> Perspective – the capacity to view things in their true relations or relative importance. Looking at an incident as one moment in history.[cxxxvi]

> Perseverance – a steady persistence in adhering to a course of action, a belief, or a purpose; steadfastness.[cxxxvii]

Leaders ensure that their attitudes and actions reflect the ideals of perspective and perseverance and are focused on achieving happiness by thinking about others. If you can begin each day with these values, then you will truly have happiness at the start of and throughout the New Year.

> Twenty years from now you will be more disappointed by the things you didn't do than by the ones you did do. So, throw off the bowlines. Sail away from the safe harbor. Catch the trade winds in your sails. Explore. Dream. Discover. – Mark Twain

CHAPTER FOUR

THE LEADERSHIP PAPERS INTERVIEWS

Becoming a leader is synonymous with becoming yourself. It is precisely that simple and it is also that difficult. – Warren Bennis

THE LEADERSHIP PAPERS INTERVIEWS

In the development of The Leadership Papers I had the privilege of interviewing individuals who demonstrate the highest qualities of leadership. The participants shared their background and history, their views on leadership, success, struggle, diversity, legacy, and more.

During the interviews, a pattern emerged. The participants shared similar values of respect, grit, drive, curiosity, humility, professionalism, commitment, and a recognition of the sacrifices of those who came before them.

These individuals embody the 5-Core Skills of Exceptional Leaders and engage in Successful Continuous Development (SCD). I am honored to provide the following profiles from these exceptional leaders.

May their words inspire your leadership journey as they have inspired mine.

Jane Camarillo, Ph.D.

Vice Provost For Student Life, Saint Mary's College Of California.

BACKGROUND

Who are you and what helped make you who you are?

I am currently a chief student affairs professional at a small liberal arts college in Northern California.

I have a Ph.D. in psychology from UCLA. My interest in psychology began in high school and I had envisioned that I would be a therapist. I completed a graduate program in social psychology and found my way into student affairs through residential life and campus housing, which supported my education.

My early life helped to make me who I am today as did my education. I am an introverted observer, the youngest in my family with two older brothers. My parents had some college, encouraged us to pursue higher education and I was fortunate to be blessed with enough intelligence to get myself into graduate school. The graduate degree helped me get my foot in the door for future promotional opportunities.

How did you get started?

I think I got started in my career by the early decisions I made after getting a BA. I made the decision to go to graduate school as a freshman in college, knowing very little about what it would take to get into graduate school, how I would pay for it, and what I would do upon graduation. Leaving my home state of Texas and going to UCLA opened my eyes to the very different paths that would be available both in career and areas of study. My interest was in altruistic behavior, helping behavior, and what motivated people to engage in it. What I didn't recognize until looking back at my experiences was that student affairs is made up of professionals who seek to support young people who are just emerging into adulthood and their independent decision making. Student affairs professionals seem mostly motivated to help young people develop into positive and productive citizens – people helping people.

In graduate school, I was on course to graduate with a Ph.D. in Social Psychology and take the next steps to becoming a faculty member in a tenure-track position at some university or college. On an annual basis, I had to find financial support to get me through graduate school and that got me into student affairs, i.e., working at the front desk of my graduate student residence hall. Being an opportunistic graduate student, I also found that if you got a job as a resident assistant, you got a single room in the residence hall, for which I applied and eventually was hired. That set me on a course to a career in student affairs. The job supported me in graduate school but was not the same as getting a job as a research assistant with a faculty member, where you would be more likely to gain experience in the craft of research psychology. It was, however, the better course for me to follow.

SUCCESS

Define Success.

I am in my late 50s now, so my definition of success is different than when I was beginning my professional career. As a young person, my definition of success was making more money than my parents and having the respect of my peers. Today, success now resonates more with John Wooden's definition: Peace of mind attained only through self-satisfaction in knowing you made the effort to do the best of which you are capable.

What was your greatest business challenge?

My greatest business challenge revolved around the decisions that had to be made in a time when resources were light and budgets fell short. Recognizing that staff and staff morale would immediately and directly be affected, my goal was to address the budget challenge by engaging the staff in the discussions on how to reduce expenses while maintaining the mission critical functions of support for students. Given the opportunity, the staff realistically addressed the challenge and reported that they felt like active partners in the enterprise through the difficult times of staff reductions. We were fortunate to be able to take advantage of vacancies rather than identifying layoffs; however, it was still difficult to see the reduction in staff and resources and begin making lemonade.

I was fortunate in a number of different ways. The institution was small, so it was possible to work with the decision makers with authority to take action. I also had problem solving leadership in my staff and strategic thinkers. Although it was not a perfect confluence of people and circumstances, it was effective to support a collaborative response to our challenge.

What is your business philosophy?

I've worked in higher education for my entire professional career, so my business has been student support and development. My best resource has been effective staff and my practice has been to invest in their professional development whenever possible, even in lean times. I feel that when you invest in your staff, it pays off in times when innovation or new directions are needed to revitalize our work. In Student Affairs, a professional must be attuned to what is confronting the next generation of young people. When my professional staff stays current with the world that will challenge our students after graduation, we succeed in preparing them to not only lead productive lives but to have meaningful lives and careers.

LEADERSHIP

What does this mean for you? Can you define it in a sentence?

Leadership is the action of anticipating, preparing, and taking decisive steps toward a shared goal.

Who represents leader/philosophy you follow?

I suspect that my own philosophy is an amalgam of very different leaders. For example, I lead most aspects of my life by the acts and the words of Jesus Christ (I'm Catholic so the influence is predictable). It guides how I treat people and how I correct myself when my interactions are difficult, whether they are personal or in business. I'm also inspired by people like Steve Jobs, an arrogant genius who successfully changed the world with his technological innovation that emphasized the aesthetic of life – color, proportion, sound. And I'm influenced by civil servants – Abraham Lincoln – who had to demonstrate wisdom while making very difficult decisions during difficult times, being motivated by what was best for "the people." I'm inspired by those in leadership who did notable things but did not become celebrities, rather changed the world or society through action – Shirley Chisolm, Ruth Bader Ginsberg, Rachel Carson.

STRUGGLE

Define struggle.

I define struggle as the conflict between ideas or (usually) two difficult solutions where the ideal is either not going to be achieved by a decision or there is a potential compromise in personal belief in one solution that may be best for the enterprise.

What have your struggles been and how have you worked through or overcome the struggle?

I have been in struggles where the decision that I had to make was not ideal for either the enterprise or for the mission of the institution (business vs. value). In these cases, I personally had to see the benefit to our students in every decision that I made or be persuaded that there was a short-term and long-term impact to the student experience. The short term may not have been as positive but would lead to a longer-term benefit for the student and for the enterprise.

DIVERSITY

Define this in your own terms.

In my business, diversity means that there is not a dominant race, ethnicity or culture but rather an environment where there are intersections of culture, race, and ethnicity. It also means variety of perspectives (often informed by culture, race, ethnicity) and ways of thinking. In higher education, investment, and biology, diversity is a key to success.

How have you managed this?

In my work, I have to create an environment where diversity can thrive, where all ideas are considered seriously, where staff do not feel isolated or like the "other." I have to look twice to assure that we consider difference rather than try to treat all the same and that we continue to learn about what students need to feel safe and open to learning.

LEGACY

What do you want to leave behind for others, what is your legacy?

I hope that in my wake, I leave a generation of professionals who feel ready to do the good work of student affairs because they worked with me. I hope they learned how to treat people fairly, to build productive alliances with colleagues, and found opportunity in every challenge. I hope they found kindness in leadership, compassion in difficult times, and growth in adversity. I hope that the professionals who worked with our organization take with them the focus that at the center of our business is the successful student.

Why is this important for you?

If I can leave a legacy of having helped professionals grow in their careers and make them more meaningful, then I have engaged in that helping behavior that brought me into the field at the beginning. It would be, as Oprah says, a full-circle moment.

QUOTE OR WORDS TO LIVE BY/ADVICE

I was in the audience during a 2005 commencement speech of Steve Jobs, which became one of my favorites. He organized it around three simple points in the excerpts here:

> Connecting the dots – you can't connect the dots looking forward; you can only connect them looking backward…believing that the dots will connect down the road will give you the confidence to follow your heart, even when it leads you off the well-worn path, and that will make all the difference.

> Love and loss – you've got to find what you love; that is as true for work as it is for your lovers… If you haven't found it yet, keep looking and don't settle.

> Death – if today were the last day of my life, would I want to do what I am about to do today? Whenever the answer has been 'no' for too many days in a row, I know I need to change something… Remembering that you are going to die is the best way I know to avoid the trap of thinking you have something to lose… Have the courage to follow your heart and intuition.

Jobs' last remark in his speech was from the back cover of the final issue of something called the *Whole Earth Catalogue*:

"Stay hungry; stay foolish." – Stanford Commencement Speech, by Steve Jobs. [https://www.youtube.com/watch?v=UF8uR6Z6KLc]

Phil Clement

Global Chief Marketing Officer, AON.

BACKGROUND

Who are you and what helped make you who you are?

Okay. I'll fill in who I am. I think I probably have drawn a lot from the places that I've lived and the people that I've lived with. My family comes from Gary, Indiana. They were part of a steel town that had a strong work ethic. My grandfather was a commercial milkman, so he delivered milk to restaurants and things of that nature. My grandmother on that side of the family was a teacher. My other grandfather worked his way up from being a bank teller to being a vice president in a small local bank. All their friends worked in the steel mills and had a strong blue-collar background. I developed a lot of respect for all these people. I would love to sit down with any of my relatives and have a conversation to compare notes, because they were just smart, capable people that I adored.

Being a part of this community helped me understand that no matter what someone is doing, they can provide leadership and a strong family base.

Then I moved to Seattle. I think that probably changed or at least allowed me to grow up in an environment where there wasn't a thing called work–life balance. It was almost the opposite of the Midwest. In the Midwest, I think, because of the manufacturing mentality, you were supposed to keep things in balance. You clocked in and clocked out, and there was a separation from work and family. Then in Seattle, you were just supposed to find something you loved and do it 24/7. If you loved coffee, you opened a coffee shop and it became Starbucks. If you liked skis, you opened a ski company and it became REI and K2.

These people didn't apologize for loving what they did. They were full-in. I picked that up as a Seattleite. Then we moved back to Chicago and I went to high school there. Probably became familiar [again] with the family ethic and that work ethic. Then college, USC, which was fun and great training. I really dug into the social sciences. I loved capturing people, so I studied visual anthropology. While at USC, an important part of my leadership journey was student government. I learned something there that motivated a lot of things for the rest of my life. I realized that I needed to pick up a quantitative skillset. I didn't have it. I decided to take it on fully and went to Chicago to study econometrics and statistics and earned two master's degrees there.

I think if you add it all up, I am someone who really believes in my roots. I believe in family. I believe in friendships. I believe that everyone really can have an impact, that's not role-specific or organization-specific or hierarchy-specific. You should find something you love and work hard at it. That idea is a mix of the things that are insightful and wonderful about people, but you've got to measure it too.

I think that probably describes me a little bit and the things that influence me quite a bit.

SUCCESS

Define Success.

I don't have a specific definition for [business or professional] success, but one place that I really did define success was with my wife about raising our kids. We wanted to do everything we could to have our children feel comfortable in their skin. Just feel good about who they are and enjoy life. Then the second success idea was that they felt a sense of empathy that motivated some responsibility. Those are the two ideas that have always been very personally important to us. I think professionally, a lot of my objectives and goals change every year.

I suppose everyone will have ideas that they sit with and reflect on. But for me to feel successful, I need to be able to help friends, family, etc., when they need it.

I don't really have a specific sense of success. I certainly have definitions of failure. A lot of them have to do with being self-centered or overly greedy. You want your presence on the planet, or in a business, or in a friendship, or in a relationship, to be a net positive, right? You don't want to take more than you give into any of those situations.

What was your greatest business challenge?

Over the years, 11 years with Aon, has been just building a great global brand that resonates in 120 countries and is something that people want to be a part of. We grew through acquisition. We have an industry that has a very high renewal rate. It's not a company that we've often worried about was just going to disappear or fail. It's always been more about reaching into our aspirations. When you've done almost 500 acquisitions, you really must make it a place where people are going to do something exciting and interesting; something that they want to be a part of. We had to build a brand. We had to build a mission around the brand and a sense of community around it. That's been a pretty consistent challenge.

I think there are a lot of reasons why some companies go the other way. The last decade has been hard. You've had to do things like change pension plans, [engage in] workforce reductions, deal with new regulations... There are lots of reasons for people not to trust a company. Leaders lie, right? The company might say one thing and do another thing. I think the biggest challenge really has been to try and create that genuine place that people want to be a part of.

What is your business philosophy?

The most consistent philosophy in all my jobs has been to create a place that people genuinely want to be a part of. When I started at Wisdom, it was a base philosophy. It was fun. We did a lot of creative new things that just hadn't been seen in that industry before. When I created my own firm, we maintained this philosophy. We engaged with our staff, we would give out awards that were passed from person to person, created ceremonies and rituals that people enjoyed. We had a great culture that people wanted to be a part of.

LEADERSHIP

What does this mean for you? Can you define it in a sentence?

I don't have one that I keep on hand. I always feel very uncomfortable talking about myself as a leader. But, I would say generically that I think of a leader as someone who can get people to go in new directions and can get folks to perform together.

In the end you must be willing to *not* be a leader or recognized as the leader *so-to-speak* [or think about being in charge or in control]. Sometimes it works and sometimes it doesn't, but you can't view leadership as a specific set of actions or a formula that works in every situation. You must adjust to the needs at the time. I find I'm effective when I'm 100% focused on contributing to a given situation and taking care of the people around me. The way you take care of others is what determines whether you are successful.

Always acknowledge that no matter the task, life is short, and people should be having fun. No amount of compensation can change that. Maybe it can for short periods of time, but I think it's important to realize that joy is one of the things people should get out of their work.

STRUGGLE

Define Struggle.

I shy away from saying that I've struggled. I have struggled running cross country, I have struggled climbing mountains, I've struggled trying to backpack across Iceland and things like that. Those were manufactured experiences because I wanted to test myself and overcome major challenges. There are people who struggle through war and hunger and political unrest. Some pretty terrible things. No matter how hard things get, I think of that and it helps me maintain perspective and optimism. Sometimes when I feel conflicted, I think back to my preparation for mountain climbing and running. I make sure that I have the right plan and that I've thought well about my equipment; and then I work hard until I come out the other side.

What have your struggles been and how have you worked through or overcome the struggle?

I think those are work challenges. At 50, I'm going to have a different perspective on this than I did when I was 20. I think there are challenges where your ego gets in the way and you just have to keep reminding yourself that that's your ego. It's not always easy, and sometimes it takes you a while to realize that [ego is] the thing that is creating the consternation or that's the thing you're battling.

For example, I can ask, "Am I going to be successful in this task?" or "Is the way I'm approaching this going to show that I did a good job?" Those kinds of things can sometimes be an element of a struggle, but if you realize again that it's not life and death, that you're usually not in a very terrible situation and that you just want to give your best to make it better, it can come out in an okay place.

I think I've always been sensitive to the folks that are going through substantial struggle.

DIVERSITY

Define this in your own terms.

I've got a lot of thoughts on diversity. I think the creative process is generally two parts. There's a divergent stage and a convergent stage. There's the time when you get a little lost and you look around for ideas and patterns and then there's a very artistic stage, where you start to build things and bring them into shape. Then you've got to go through formal decisions on what's a good idea and then execute the plan. Every stage of creativity brings different perspectives and is unbelievably helpful to success. Myopia is always problematic. I just inherently love the notion of coming at any problem or any strategy, or execution, from many different perspectives. Diversity is one of the great ways to do that.

We could certainly talk immediately about ethnic diversity and educational diversity, but there's so many. Age diversity, sex diversity, orientation diversity. Obviously, it goes on to discipline and learning styles and academic background. I think the more you can get the diverse point of view, the better off you are at all those stages. There's also that notion of joy at work and work ethic. If you only acknowledge 60% of a person, I think you're only going to get 60% of them at work. When people can bring all of themselves to work with all their points of view, and can be part of a community, that changes how they engage and what they give the job. What I'd love to see is people totally passionate about what's going on. I think embracing diversity is a big part of making that possible.

I've been particularly involved in LGBT issues recently because I just see it as an important frontier. When you push on that one, it brings a lot of other issues with it.

If you start to work with an increased acceptance of transgender people in the workplace, it brings with it a lot of understanding of gender issues. You recognize that people are fully human with things going on in their lives outside of the workplace that are important. It's one of those great issues and that's one of the reasons I push on that one.

LEGACY

What do you want to leave behind for others, what is your legacy?

It starts with our kids, right? I hope I can continue to succeed in the goals that I set out for them; empathy and self-confidence. Then I can go a little bit wider. I generally hope that humanity continues to be on a positive course and that I can contribute to that positively. That's a big sense of legacy, and it's certainly not about any amount of money made. It's certainly not a building. You know what I mean? You just want to feel like you helped. I think that's probably it.

I have a more mature version of the idea of legacy now. It would have been interesting to ask me this question every decade.

QUOTE OR WORDS TO LIVE BY/ADVICE

When it comes to marketing, I always say, "There's so many things you can do, so if you can't measure it, don't do it."

There are things I tell my children. The version of "It doesn't matter if you win or lose. It's how you play the game." What I really say is, "It doesn't matter if you win or lose as long as people on your team want to be on your team again."

Of course, my oldest always said "Well why would they want to be on my team again if I lose?" Good point. I don't know. It's all situational wisdom that mostly my parents said.

"Too late to make a friend when you need one." "Now is exactly the time you can choose not to get even."

Sarah Goldstein Herman, Esq.

Managing Partner Of The Orange County Office Of O'Hagan Meyer.

BACKGROUND

Who are you and what helped make you who you are?

I am the Employment Law Practice Group Leader at my firm. I'm responsible for business development and case administration. I attribute who I am to [a] lot of hard work/long hours, following my heart and interests and being in the right place at the right time.

How did you get started?

I almost didn't! I wanted to join the Peace Corps after law school but now I'm glad I decided to try practicing law. I didn't go to a "top tier" law school and I didn't have a ton of job offers out of school. I worked as a temporary legal secretary until I got my bar results and I worked at a local bookstore on nights and weekends. My first law job paid modestly—not like one of these $170,000 first-year salaries that keep making the papers lately. I worked a lot of hours and wasn't sure I loved law until I got my first employment law case and VOILA! It was like a light bulb went on above my head. I loved employment law – I love the facts and getting to know people and helping employers.

SUCCESS

Define Success.

That's such a tough question! I think each person has to define that for themselves. I also think it's a question that should be revisited often. Having a family really changed the definition of success for me. It's not an option to fail as a wife and mother. Suddenly I had more than just work goals to worry about fulfilling. My definition of success has never been about money. I think the most important commodity is time and how you spend it. Spending time on things I love and with people I love is time well spent. Time well spent leads to a life well lived and that is success for me. I like to achieve goals – each year I set 10 personal and professional goals – obtain 2 new clients; teach my son to use "please and thank you" appropriately; get to yoga four times a month. This is how I build life balance into my measure of achievement and success. On the business side, I push for revenue but never at the expense of a good result for my client. I could do better financially if I pushed all my cases to trial – but that won't yield the best result for my clients, so I make sure my clients know about all of their options and we settle cases when it's a better business decision for them.

What was your greatest business challenge?

When I was younger, I had a harder time being taken seriously. Growing a few gray hairs helped a lot.

What is your business philosophy?

Sorry I don't have a short phrase that sums it up – I believe in truly partnering with clients to achieve results.

LEADERSHIP

What does this mean for you? Can you define it in a sentence?

The ability to inspire another person to greatness.

Who represents leader/philosophy you follow?

I don't have one in particular that I follow. I listen to a lot of TED Talks during drive time looking for inspiration on how to be a better leader. I'm constantly working to improve communications and looking for better ways to inspire.

STRUGGLE

Define struggle.

A struggle is an obstacle holding you back. All lawsuits are problems that need to be resolved. In business, problems/struggles come up all the time. Your ability to move forward depends on your ability to solve problems.

What have your struggles been and how have you worked through or overcome the struggle?

I struggle with wanting to praise associates for a job well done and asking them to make changes in their writing or arguments to assist with improvement. I feel that if I don't point out the things that could be better, I'm not helping them to improve and we aren't putting out our best product. But if I ask for too many changes it feels critical and can erode confidence. I've been lucky enough to work with a coach in the past on this issue and I continue to work on it.

DIVERSITY

Define this in your own terms.

Anyone that has a different experience, background, knowledge and/or ideology from your own.

How have you managed this?

Diversity is the cornerstone of a successful group. Incorporation of people who view a case differently add value to the evaluation and analysis. Someone once told me that an employment law group should "look like a box of Crayolas" and I agree for many reasons.

LEGACY

What do you want to leave behind for others, what is your legacy?

I want to be a good example of how you can have a family and a successful career in law. They aren't mutually exclusive.

Why is this important for you?

I see too many younger women attorneys leaving the profession or struggling with advancement at their firms. I refuse to give up my career and practice that I spent 16 years building to feel like an adequate wife and mother and I refuse to fail my family. I want women lawyers to know they have choices – they can have a career and a family. I respect stay-at-home moms (in fact, I think it looks a ton harder than my job) but I don't like to hear of women leaving the profession because they felt they had no choice. I do my absolute best to coach young female attorneys and I hire women returning to their careers after they took time with kids at home. These women are brilliant and hardworking and have a lot to contribute.

QUOTE OR WORDS TO LIVE BY/ADVICE

"Everyone is responsible for their own fun" – it really applies to all kinds of situations; personal responsibility and empowerment to change things about your life or yourself; don't look to someone else to make things better for you – it's your show – it's your deal, you do it! And my mother says, "anything worth doing is worth doing well."

Jana Hunter

Owner, Two Hunters Productions, A Loan Out Company.

BACKGROUND

Who are you and what helped make you who you are?

Born in Durham, NC. Traditional family unit (Mother, Father, two siblings). K-12 in Durham City public schools. High school was a magnet program. University of North Carolina – BS in Dental Hygiene (my father thought it was important to have a fall back career. He wasn't wrong).

I am an outgoing, plain-spoken southern gal who looks at the world through humor goggles. I have a dental hygiene degree that I rarely use (only occasionally when a friend thinks they are getting ripped off by their dentist and I read the X-rays for him/her) and have spent the last twenty years writing for TV sitcoms – rising to the somewhat meaningless title of Executive Producer. I always had to be the clown. I was obese before it was cool. As the fat kid, I prided myself on beating everybody to the joke about me before they could get to it – volunteering to be the receptionist in a game of doctor. In school, countless teachers would tell me to get more serious about their subject or I wouldn't amount to much. Ha. I'd love to go back and show them that "smart ass" has a great paying job.

My family most certainly helped shape the person I am. My father was a stern taskmaster. He expected a lot out of you, and you met those expectations or suffer the consequences. But he was also one of the funniest guys I have ever met, and I attribute my sense of humor to him. Getting a real, genuine laugh out of him was awesome and became my life's work. My mother was one of the first female TV reporters/anchorwomen in the country. I spent a great deal of my childhood at WTVD and realized that TV and all things TV were my passions – except journalism. I was almost a chip off the old block. Seeing a strong independent woman like my mom made me realize I wasn't locked into the old girl stereotypes. My husband was the piece of the puzzle that made it all come together. I was used to being the funniest person in the room till I met Mitch. He is hilarious but at the time unfocused. My determination and his mad comedy skills – well success was a given.

How did you get started?

Mitch [my husband and writing partner] and I both knew we had to pursue show business – HAD TO. It wasn't something we just thought might be fun. We lived it. I started out in the Groundlings program and Mitch took sitcom writing classes in the evenings at UCLA Extension. I went on to do stand-up and take acting classes from a hot shot coach named Howard Fine. As we progressed in our separate worlds, I would ask Mitch if he thought my writing was funny and he asked me if his stuff was funny and pretty soon, we were writing partners. We woke up in the mornings and wrote before work. We came home from our jobs and wrote till midnight. We finally wrote a "Grace Under Fire" script that landed us in the Warner Brothers writers' workshop. And while we didn't get jobs out of the program, we became better writers. We went on to write a "King of The Hill" spec script that caught some heat and landed us our first job. "Holding The Baby" – a show that my mother just loved.

SUCCESS

Define Success.

My father used to say: "The harder I work, the luckier I get." I believe this with all my heart. But that being said: success is whatever you think it is. I don't think success is just about making money. Success is about getting out there every day, being productive and really enjoying yourself. I once was leaving a parking garage and encountered the happiest person ever taking money in the booth. Was he making a ton of money? I doubt it. Was he successful? Absolutely! He was the best darn parking garage attendant I have ever met. Are you mostly happy? Do you have love in your life? Do you have family and friends around? If you answered yes to any of that, you're successful!

What was your greatest business challenge?

When you pursue a life in the arts, always your biggest challenge is finding an outlet – where can I put on my play or sketch show? Who will hire me to write for them? How can I get money to fund my project? It's a crazy competitive business for very limited resources. But if I can do it, it ain't impossible.

What is your business philosophy?

NEVER, NEVER, EVER, EVER GIVE UP. There will always be naysayers! Don't listen to them and don't do the MATH. If you start thinking about the odds, you're dead already.

LEADERSHIP

What does this mean for you? Can you define it in a sentence?

It's funny I think of the leader as the person out in front, leading the charge, making it all happen, dodging the first bullets. I feel like I'm more the person in the middle of the charge and I only become the leader if everybody else goes down in front of me – which hopefully they won't. I'm very comfortable with this position – some responsibility but not all the responsibility. Second banana in a sitcom is the job we should all be shooting for – you don't carry the show like the star but it's still fun and pays well. I'd be cool with that.

Who/what represents a leader/philosophy you follow?

Don't be mad but I kind of hate all that crap – people writing books on their success. It's a damn site easier to Lean In, Cheryl Sandberg, with a house full of help than when you're a single mom working an office job. I suppose though I would definitely consider my mom, Martie Johnson, a leader I followed. She was a female pioneer in the field of TV journalism and that's really something when you think about it. I guess I'm sort of a pioneer. I'm not the first female sitcom writer but there still aren't that many. I have frequently been the only gal in the room.

STRUGGLE

Define struggle.

Not being true to yourself. I find that many of my struggles have come when I denied who I am and what I really want out of life. I thought a career in show business was an insane pursuit and I attempted to take a safer route with a dental hygiene degree and finding corporate jobs that were "stable." It just wasn't my world and I knew it. My first day in a writers' room, I knew these were my people and I had found Valhalla.

What have your struggles been and how have you worked through or overcome the struggle?

I have been lucky in my life and I wouldn't compare my struggles to say someone living in a cardboard city in Rio or a hovel in Bangladesh. Those people truly struggle. My parents afforded me a comfortable life and a college degree. But out of college, I wasn't quite prepared for life and I got myself in some debt problems – I cut up all my credit cards and lived off my meager salary (by picking up a second job) but got everything paid back. Also, when Mitch and I first came out to LA, debt reared its ugly head again and we found ourselves in tremendous debt. Belief in yourself can often be expensive, not to mention life in LA. Luckily, we scored an apartment manager job (lowering our rent) and soon after that broke into show business. Through hard work, again, we paid it all back. There really are no shortcuts. Nose to the grindstone is once again the answer to overcoming struggles. Also, good old-fashioned hard work distracts you and you don't realize you're struggling. As a woman, balance between career and home. This struggle is as old as women have been allowed to work. I chose not to have a child till I felt I could afford one so that helped but now I am the 50-year-old mother with the 30–40 something set. My only regret about that is not adopting more kids. I just never had much confidence in myself as a mother.

DIVERSITY

Define this in your own terms.

Different people from all backgrounds – differing faiths, races, cultures, sexual orientation and gender identities, etc., coming together with a common goal – to go after, life, liberty, and the pursuit of happiness. Oh, also, the hopes that these people would share their differences and others would be open to learn about the differences till they are no longer perceived as different. Is this even close?

How have you managed this?

I went to a multi-cultural high school and then moved to LA. My daughter attends a multi-cultural school. I try to treat everyone with respect and dignity. I adopted a child from China. I pay my nanny full-time for a part-time job in hopes that makes raising her daughter easier. I also provide dental, medical, and vet care (she has two dogs) as needed…

LEGACY

What do you want to leave behind for others, what is your legacy?

500 30-minute episodes of TV and an amazing daughter who contributes to society. She'd better anyway. The Middle is certainly something I am proud of. It is a clean show that the whole family can watch, and it is shocking because it isn't violent and filthy.

Why is this important for you?

It's not really. …Unless you're Stephen Hawking or Einstein or somebody like that – how long is anything anybody did going to last? In this fast-paced world of Internet and social media, everyone is always looking for the next new thing and people seldom look back to appreciate the great old thing.

QUOTE OR WORDS TO LIVE BY/ADVICE

I have a few things that work for me. I used to chant: "There is no spoon." It is a line from the Matrix and whenever I got scared or overwhelmed, I would chant that to myself. It just meant that everything is an allusion and somehow, I took comfort in that. "The harder I work, the luckier I get." Aristotle has this great quote: "We are what we repeatedly do. Excellence, then, is not an act, but a habit." Eleanor Roosevelt suggests that "We do the thing we think we cannot do." My advice is to work harder at what you love than you think is humanly possible and be open to anything. Love yourself, your family, and friends. And use the deathbed test when you are unsure of anything. Nobody on their deathbed says, "I wish I wouldn't have tried so hard, I wish I wouldn't have taken that trip and experienced life, I wish I had bought less iCloud storage, etc." You get the idea.

Alan Jenkins, Esq.

President, The Opportunity Agenda.

BACKGROUND

Who are you and what helped make you who you are?

I am a father, a husband, a son, a brother, a lawyer, a communicator, a social justice leader. My parents – both teachers and activists – had the greatest influence on my life choices and commitment to justice for all. But I was fortunate to have many mentors and role models, from teachers and bosses to my law school mate Barack Obama. I've also had a wealth of experiences and opportunities, at a global philanthropic foundation and the U.S. Supreme Court, and with grassroots leaders and desperately poor residents in the U.S. and around the world. All those experiences shaped who I am and continue to do so.

How did you get started?

I got started as a college intern at the American Civil Liberties Union.

SUCCESS

Define Success.

Supporting and enjoying family while making the world a better place.

What was your greatest business challenge?

Creating a unique new organization of a kind that had never existed before.

What is your business philosophy?

Treat everyone in the organization as if they might one day run the organization.

LEADERSHIP

What does this mean for you? Can you define it in a sentence?

The vision, values, and commitment to inspire and empower others.

Who represents leader/philosophy you follow?

Anthony Romero, ACLU.

STRUGGLE

Define struggle.

Tackling obstacles that challenge your very identity.

What have your struggles been and how have you worked through or overcome the struggle?

My early struggles involved being the only African American in most of my classes, jobs, and so many other settings. I worked through them by working harder and achieving higher standards than most of those around me. My later struggles have involved balancing work and family. I've been intentional about that – for example, in 10 years at my organization, I've gone into the office on a weekend exactly zero times.

DIVERSITY

Define this in your own terms.

Diversity is the idea that people of different backgrounds, experiences, and perspectives can solve problems and generate ideas that a homogeneous group could never produce. It is that profoundly American ideal of E Pluribus Unum – Out Of Many, One.

How have you managed this?

I don't see diversity as something to manage. I have benefited from diversity in my work and life by developing fluency across communities and finding ways for people with different skills and perspectives to work together effectively.

LEGACY

What do you want to leave behind for others, what is your legacy?

I hope that my legacy is as a loving and supportive father, husband, son, and brother, and as someone who left our country and world better than he found it.

Why is this important for you?

It's what gives my life meaning.

QUOTE OR WORDS TO LIVE BY/ADVICE

Be the change you want to see in the world – Gandhi.

John P. Keil, Esq.

Partner, Collazo Florentino & Keil LLP.

BACKGROUND

Who are you and what helped make you who you are?

People usually meet me as an attorney advising and representing management on labor and employment matters, or as husband and father to my family, or through involvement in my church. I've occasionally introduced myself as a classical trumpet player.

I more often think of myself in terms of my interests and hobbies, which comprise an embarrassingly long list ranging from linguistics to mycology to data analysis, or in terms of various idiosyncratic characteristics. I insist, for example, on precision in language and logic, I have a knack for putting into words the complex emotional and interpersonal matters of others, and I have an incurable tendency to provide exhaustive answers to innocent questions.

How did you get started?

As a child, I had a very supportive home environment, and my parents did everything within their means to support me as I pursued different interests and obtained attractive academic credentials. Only as an adult did I start to understand just how much else they did for me, often teaching me by example or even by omission, as they shared the best that they had learned and shielded me from the worst that they'd experienced. I was also lucky to have a number of very good public-school teachers, music teachers, and supportive people in the community when I was growing up.

Although I studied philosophy in college, I became dissatisfied with what I considered the insular habits of academia and concluded that studying law could help me understand the world in a way that philosophy had not. Professionally, I got my start when I was looking for gainful employment after law school, and Ernest Collazo, Frank Carling, and Risa Mish decided to hire me to work in their law firm, despite my not having taken a single course in labor law or employment law. They gave me extraordinary opportunities, as did Tonianne Florentino when she joined the firm as a partner a short time later. Years later, my name ended up on the door.

SUCCESS

Define Success.

Unless we have in mind the attainment of a specific goal, I think we have to define success as growing enough beyond our current set of challenges to embrace something more ambitious. In doing so, of course, we need to make sure we remain whole people, sacrificing neither our needs, our values, or our relationships in the pursuit of fulfillment.

What was your greatest business challenge?

My greatest business challenge has been learning to translate my professional skills into business propositions in a way I considered compatible with my standards of personal integrity. Perhaps because of some frustrating experiences at the receiving end of sales pitches, for quite a long time I resisted making sales pitches, and was embarrassed by the amount I needed to charge for my professional advice. In addition, although I eventually came to understand that there are methods for bringing in business, these were never obvious to me and also never explicitly taught, until I hired a business coach to give me personalized guidance. Acquiring a clearer perspective on these points has been an essential part of my growth as a professional.

What is your business philosophy?

I would be uncomfortable saying that how I run my business should be any different from how I live my life in general. Clients, adversaries, judges, professional colleagues, and others all have to be able to know that I can be counted on to mean what I say and to deliver what I promise, and that I will not work to undermine the truth, a just outcome, or anyone's personal dignity. Nearly everyone, I believe, wants to do the right thing, even if they disagree about what that is or how to achieve it, and clients generally seek out my guidance because they want my help in unraveling these questions.

LEADERSHIP

What does this mean for you? Can you define it in a sentence?

Leadership means formulating and sharing a vision of the greater good, motivating others to work toward the same (or at least overlapping) goals, and having the character, judgment, and interpersonal skills to guide the enterprise in times of doubt and moral challenge. I've come to realize, however, that good leadership does not necessarily mean having all the answers, or even necessarily sharing them if you think you do, as that can encourage dependency. An important part of leadership is recognizing that delegating can encourage participation and pride of ownership, even if the result may no longer resemble our own vision for the outcome. Knowing where to strike that balance, in my view, is an important part of leadership.

Who/what represents a leader/philosophy you follow?

I think it would be a mistake to idolize specific historical figures. All great leaders have had some personal failings, or at the very least shared the limitations of their time and place in history. It would also be a mistake to assume that we could imitate their paths to success – not only are the factors contributing to their success far more numerous (and subject to chance) than people ordinarily assume, but I suspect that most great leaders, like the rest of us, make things up as they go along more often than they might care to admit. They may be exercising great care and wisdom in reaching their decisions, but they are still coping with great uncertainty at nearly every turn, and their successes may not be reproducible.

I have, however, long been interested in the early Greek philosopher Thales, who is said by some to have coined the ancient adage to "know thyself." As told in Aristotle's Politics, Thales, who was mocked for his frugal life, studied the world around him and concluded that there would be a bountiful olive crop in the coming season. He then bought all the olive presses so that when the crop was ready, he had a monopoly on the production of olive oil; Aristotle concluded from this that Thales could turn things to his advantage if he chose, but had set his mind to loftier tasks. Plato, in his dialogue Theaetetus, has Socrates relate a parallel story: that Thales may have been widely mocked for falling into a ditch when he had his eyes on the stars above, and was useless in discussions of gossip and trivia, but was precisely the guide one would wish for while struggling with deeper questions. I find the example of Thales interesting, not because of his success on any particular occasion, but because of the clarity of his priorities.

A different way to answer the same question would be to consider the writers and thinkers I have turned to for guidance during dark periods. Although their writings may not encompass a specific philosophy, and they as individuals were also not without flaws, Montaigne's Essays and Seneca's Letters offer much to think about, and I might consider their observations on life before I copied the conduct of specific historical figures.

STRUGGLE

Define struggle.

The word "struggle" may have historical overtones, and to my ear implies a continuing lack of success; I prefer to frame my response in terms of challenges. I like to think of challenges as things that are worth doing, generally because they bring us closer to a certain objective, but do not come easily. Considered another way, I am mindful of William James's observation that the great philosophical problems are never solved, so much as outgrown.

What have your struggles been and how have you worked through or overcome the struggle?

I consider myself fortunate in many ways – I have enjoyed good health, supportive and happy family life, good friends, and the opportunity to explore fulfilling interests, among a great many other blessings and advantages. If we accept Heraclitus's aphorism that our character is our fate, my challenges have arguably been almost entirely problems of my own creation. Rather than cataloguing all my faults, I will offer comments on a few, in the hope that someone might find something to value in my comments.

One of my biggest challenges in life has been in learning to manage worry – training myself, for example, to recognize in the moment that rehearsing the parade of terrible but perhaps unlikely disasters that could befall me or my loved ones is not a constructive way to live my life. An early insight came when I realized that as I approached a dreaded event, the facts at hand could no longer support my worries. Instead of calming down, I tended to transfer my worries to some later event that I could perceive less clearly. In other words, the event itself was not the source of my anxiety, but an outlet for it, and I, not the world around me, was the source of this emotional agitation. When we always worry, our concerns do turn out to be correct once in a while. Even here, I came to recognize that in the handful of cases where something awful did happen, I have, though perhaps with misgivings, learned to adapt.

Ever since those first observations, I have been trying to identify other sources of worry – such as the recurring concern that doing or saying the wrong thing would ruin a relationship. Here it was pointed out to me (by my wife) that my fear of rejection was a horrible slight to the character of the people around me, all of them warm, forgiving, trusting, compassionate, and altogether remarkable human beings. It was startling to realize that nearly all of my reluctance to engage others was based entirely on anticipated rejections and confrontations that never came to pass.

I have also always worried about being good enough – not just skilled enough, smart enough, or articulate enough, but brave enough, and even moral enough, to justify the trust being placed in me. There is, of course, no substitute for the study, practice, and brutal self-criticism required for peak accomplishments. Over time I have learned to tame my fear of failure by acknowledging that all of us, at some point, have to improvise. Hopefully our judgment will be right, but it will inevitably sometimes miss the mark, and we will rarely have all the time and information required for a perfect solution; that is simply the nature of professional work. More fundamentally, I realized at some point that it was foolish for me to measure my abilities and accomplishments according to conventional standards. This was not simply recognizing that happiness would always be out of reach if it were allowed to depend on things beyond my control; rather, it was discovering after decades of watching the people around me that my mind just did not function in the same way that most others' did: that what seemed easy, obvious or interesting to them was often not so for me, and the reverse; and that these differences did not mean that there was anything amiss with me, or anything to apologize for. Thus, I learned not to measure myself against socially prescribed standards of excellence, but against my own. This could easily become an excuse to shun the world, because human beings are occasionally such baffling, infuriating, or terrifying creatures. But the composer Arnold Schoenberg observed that the point of art was not to make people comfortable, and I concluded that a life that was entirely comfortable, much like Socrates's unexamined life, might not have much worth, so I decided instead to study the people around me, the better to engage and learn from them.

DIVERSITY

Define this in your own terms.

The philosopher and psychologist William James observed that a complete system of ethics could never be worked out entirely in advance, because all the claims of humanity could not be anticipated and settled until the end of time, when all is fully known. Diversity, which seems to have emerged as a value relatively recently in our history, is only one example of a value that early statesmen, lawmakers, and philosophers failed to predict, and is unlikely to be the last; we simply can't imagine or identify all of the norms and practices we take for granted today that may be considered despicable a few centuries from now. I'm also mindful that there is some inconsistency in how diversity is defined: some seem to reserve the concept specifically in terms of correcting certain past injustices, and some seem to prioritize numerical representation for its own sake in a manner that may be hard to distinguish from quotas. In recent years, we have also seen notions such as micro-aggressions and safe spaces receiving greater attention, which suggests that, at least for some, the idea may still be evolving.

Underlying many notions of diversity is the sometimes-unstated premise that diversity is a moral value, and not simply a practical one. If it is a moral value, then it follows not only that people should be held accountable only for what they can control, that the process of striving for diversity should be the focus of our attention rather than the results in any particular case, which are so often governed by chance, and that our process should be regarded as fair and as consistent with our other moral values. If it is to retain traction as a moral imperative, diversity cannot be a partisan concept, as it sometimes seems today.

If this perspective is correct, then I'm concerned that some of the ways in which diversity is presented as a value today do not leave enough room for other values, such as trust and compassion. As I try to point out in my advice and training programs on the subject, no corporate policy can cause people to trust one another, but that is precisely what is needed. With the particularly strained race and cross-cultural relations we've seen in recent years, some caution is understandable; it is difficult to show trust and practice compassion when you feel threatened. But if we are to grow wiser as a society, we will have [to] learn to treat diversity as a consistent process, not as a series of results we regard as favorable or unfavorable, and not as something that depends on the composition of a particular applicant pool, or even a set of favored social categories, that will inevitably evolve over time. For diversity to be effective as a moral imperative, I suspect its practitioners will have to learn to see everyone else as unique individuals, rather than merely as representatives of particular groups. This is not easy to do; it may well be an unavoidable element of how our minds work that knowing a few seemingly arbitrary details about a person generates the illusion that we know and understand them, that we can predict their behavior in hypothetical circumstances, and that we understand them better than they could possibly understand us. In most cases, it may simply never occur to us that there could be anything further to know about them. But knowing more about one another is essential, because the broader our perspective, the more compassionate and inclusive we can become.

If this line of reasoning is sound, then it seems to me that diversity, as a value, should be defined as striving to understand and overcome the limitations of our perceptions of one another, so that we are continually learning better how to trust and be trusted, to show and receive compassion, and to continually expand and enrich our perspective to include, with ever-greater detail, the points of view of others.

How have you managed this?

I think it would be a mistake to assert that diversity is something that can be definitively "achieved;" like many other desirable states, it may be more of a process than an achievement. The way that I personally have invested the most time reaching toward diversity is through self-instruction – researching extensively how and why people behave the way they do, trying to understand how we stumble unaware into false conclusions, considering the meaning and implications of the implicit attitude test, and other topics. At some point, of course, we have to put what we learn into practice, and I do this by writing and speaking about what I've learned, helping to promote suitably inclusive policies, guiding clients as they struggle with these issues, and continually nudging myself to engage with others.

LEGACY

What do you want to leave behind for others, what is your legacy?

I would hope, as a father, to give my children what they need to be happy in life and to share that happiness with others. That achievement would be more than enough to consider my life lived well.

Why is this important for you?

If we can reasonably claim more than that, I would like to leave the world a happier, healthier, more peaceful, better understood place than I found it.

QUOTE OR WORDS TO LIVE BY/ADVICE

The Stoic philosopher Epictetus observed that people who do something to harm us are often acting out of a misplaced sense of duty. I have often used this as a starting point when trying to create an opening for kindness and compassion in times of anger, exasperation, or distress.

Niloufer Pabla

Managing Partner, Niloufer A. Pabla, CPA, An Accountancy Corporation.

BACKGROUND

Who are you and what helped make you who you are?

I love developing connections with people and causing change. I value respect, integrity, commitment, perseverance, and I have deep appreciation for all those who have helped me become the person I am today. My life experiences, including all my relationships, the good ones and all the bad ones, have helped me become the person I am today.

How did you get started?

By being born. Every day of life is an opportunity to make a difference. After seeing the struggles of my mother, a single parent raising four children, I decided at a very young age that the only way I was going to make a change in this cycle was to get a college education which would help me get a good paying job. This is where my perseverance and commitment were born. I was able to put myself through college while working full time and graduated with honors. That level of perseverance and commitment didn't end there; I still own it!

SUCCESS

Define Success.

For me, success is not only meeting the goals you set for yourself, but also maintaining your morals and values while doing so.

What was your greatest business challenge?

Creating a non-profit organization which helps in shaping the financial mindset for individuals from youth through adulthood.

What is your business philosophy?

Always be willing to learn more and share what you learn; recognize your strengths and opportunities for the betterment of yourself and others; take calculated risks; not only manage people but help them develop.

LEADERSHIP

What does this mean for you? Can you define it in a sentence?

Lead by example; treat others how you want to be treated.

Who/what represents a leader/philosophy you follow?

Anyone who inspires to achieve the impossible, by doing it themselves. Rosa Parks, Martin Luther King, Jr., Mother Teresa, Nelson Mandela are a few of the greatest.

STRUGGLE

Define struggle.

A struggle is an experience that is beyond your capacity at that point in time, or an experience that is not in line with your personal values, at that point in time.

What have your struggles been and how have you worked through or overcome the struggle?

A flexible mind, education, and a desire to make change have been key to overcoming my struggles. I am not talking about a degree from an institution of higher education. I am referencing the ability to recognize that I am experiencing a struggle and taking that in a positive manner, with a flexible mind, to actively listen to the other side to better understand and educate myself so I can move forward in successfully executing an effective solution to my struggle.

My early struggles involved beating all odds to not only get into college but staying in college and graduating! I worked through these struggles by researching and tapping into every resource that was available to me for the circumstances I was in. I stayed connected to those who had achieved the same goal despite all the obstacles they also had to face.

DIVERSITY

Define this in your own terms.

Being exposed to and influenced by all the different categories that humans may fall into, including race, gender, age, religion, sexual orientation, ethnicity, culture, etc.

How have you managed this?

By simply being open in all possible ways and reflecting on what I can learn from a particular experience: having an open mind without having any possible initial judgments influence my mind, open ears to actively listen and learn, and an open door for anyone who may want to engage in a relationship. I take this openness one step further and try to go out of my comfort zone into new atmospheres that I may initially feel nervous about, which usually is an educational experience for me. I think it is equally important to speak out and share my experiences with others to help provide diversity to other people.

LEGACY

What do you want to leave behind for others, what is your legacy?

Inspire to cause a positive and constructive change. Be open to learning, including learning from other people while still maintaining your values, and lead by example by treating others how you want to be treated.

Why is this important for you?

It gives my life meaning. Too many times, we limit our own growth by not being open-minded. If we each were to reach our full potential, imagine how happy we would make ourselves and how happy we'd make the people around us simply by the virtue of me being happier that I can provide more to the world.

QUOTE OR WORDS TO LIVE BY/ADVICE

Be the change you wish to see in the world. - Gandhi

Sukhi S. Pabla

CAO Revolution Entertainment Services, And Co-Founder, P2 Films.

BACKGROUND

Who are you and what helped make you who you are?

Who am I? This is an interesting question. It is interesting because there is a social me, a cultural me, a professional me, and there is the internal me. Socially, I am a father, a husband, a brother, a son, and a friend. Professionally, a business owner, a writer, a film producer. Culturally, a Punjabi-born – Sikh, that doesn't practice the religion but still listens to only Indian music while raised in America. The truth is that I am a father because I have a son. I am a husband because I have a wife. An entertainment industry expert because I chose the profession. A person that likes certain things because of when and where I was born. So, all my identities, everything I believe myself to be, are all dependent on something else. So then, who am I? A father, a husband, an entertainment professional, all the above or something else?

The answer is I am none of the above. I am just a passenger that likes to smell the roses. And learning about people and their experiences helped make me who I am.

How did you get started?

I was born.

SUCCESS

Define Success.

Being able to do what I want, when I want, how I want, and helping others obtain the same.

What was your greatest business challenge?

Leaving a comfortable job and starting a business was the biggest challenge. Having a business will always have its own challenges. But having a business is the biggest challenge.

What is your business philosophy?

My business philosophy is no different than my own life philosophy. The lesson that took me the longest to learn is that you have to help people to get what you want. Business is all about relationships, and you can't keep asking people for favors without repaying them.

I've also learned that if I help people, they will go an extra mile to help me. And if I help people without expecting anything in return, people will go [an] extra ten miles to help me.

Keep paying it forward by helping everyone out there (customers, friends, family) ... no matter how big or small they may be. Sooner or later, the universe will pay it back ten-fold.

LEADERSHIP

What does this mean for you? Can you define it in a sentence?

Such a simple question, and yet it continues to vex popular consultants and lay people alike.

Leadership means different things to different people around the world, and different things in different situations. For example, it could relate to community leadership, religious leadership, political leadership, and leadership of campaigning groups.

Leadership isn't management, it's not about personal attributes, and titles don't mean anything. Live and behave in such a way that people will choose to follow you and doing so will influence their lives in a positive way.

Who represents leader/philosophy you follow?

There are so many people. I would say that any person that is willing to give his or her own life for the betterment of society is a leader that I admire. It could be Bhagat Singh, Dr. Martin Luther King, Jr., or Hiroo Onoda.

STRUGGLE

Define struggle.

I could say that it's the opposite of how I define success. Not being able to do what I want, when I want, and how I want. Truth of the matter is – for most people – there is no struggle. I am here to say, I have not struggled. I have failed, but not struggled. I have had to work hard – but not struggle. I have been broke, but not struggled. I have been laughed at, but not struggled. Everyone can define struggle differently. Unless I've been forced to do something against my will – it is not struggle. Blacks as a race struggled. A mother living in a tent in Iran with three children without a father is struggle. Child labor is struggle.

Nothing in business is struggle.

What have your struggles been and how have you worked through or overcome the struggle?

I have not had any struggles. I've only had small failures.

DIVERSITY

Define this in your own terms.

Everyone, of all races, gender, age, size, and viewpoints allowed to work together for a common goal.

How have you managed this?

I do not look at any of these listed above when choosing who I work with.

LEGACY

What do you want to leave behind for others, what is your legacy?

I want people to understand that there is nothing they must do. A lot of our society or rather human existence is about what people "have to do" to fit in. Must believe in God. Must wear clothes. Must have education. Must not be anti-social. I believe in "Live and let live."

Why is this important for you?

[Because] life is too short man.

QUOTE OR WORDS TO LIVE BY/ADVICE

I believe in "Live and let live."

I know these thoughts above are not confined to the world of business. But to me, when a person starts a business, the business has tendencies to behave in the manner the person behaves. They can become one and the same over time. It's important to know who you are as a person, because your business will become just like you. Be a successful human, and the business success will follow.

Lucille Renwick

Vice President, Fenton.

BACKGROUND

Who are you and what helped make you who you are?

I will answer with the basics and the obvious first, I am an African American working mother of three who has spent her career working on social justice issues through a variety of positions – journalist, editor, small-schools advocate, communications consultant.

There are a number of things (and people) that helped make me who I am: Parents willing to make sacrifices so I could receive a good education and be exposed to culture and different opportunities. Relatives who held positions to which I could either aspire or learn about the types of jobs and opportunities (careers) available to me. Teachers who saw potential and possibility in me and, more importantly, knew how to encourage me. My own curiosity and drive to want to learn more, do more, be more. Older siblings who refused to settle for less and encouraged me to strive for more. A realization at a young age of what I wanted to do as a career (thanks to an encouraging teacher who told me that I had talent in writing) and then realizing later that I had transferable skills that could take me in different directions – not being limited to one career path.

How did you get started?

I got internships during college at newspapers and got a huge boost from the then Times Mirror Corp.'s METPRO program for young, emerging journalists of color. That started me in journalism at the Los Angeles Times and gave me the confidence boost I needed. However, for me, more important than just getting started is having people around you and supporting you to keep you going. It is easy to get discouraged, to let those voices inside your head get the better of you. Having a network of mentors, guides, touchstones of people to call on to give you that boost of confidence is essential in one's success – no matter the field. This pool of mentors should include people above you (in age and professional experience), below you, peers, etc., but all with your best interest at heart (and vice versa). This network is key, and something often overlooked or not valued enough.

SUCCESS

Define Success.

I continue to struggle with this definition and even at this stage of my life and career, I grapple with the societal norms of success and with my personal definition of success. There is still a strong part of me (that voice in my head) that determines success by the title and position and elevation of one's status in their work – Chief Communications Officer; commencement speaker; VP; CEO, etc. Are you sought after as a leader in your field? What power and influence do you have?

Think of it: The question we are always asked after our names is 'What do you do?' And a person's facial expressions will alter depending on the answer. School teacher? We give a nice nod and 'Oh, that's interesting?' Investment banker? We are intrigued. The person who has money is 'smart.' Journalist? Respectable and intriguing enough. Homemaker?

As an African American woman who attended fairly "elite" higher-education institutions, this definition above is even more important.

But as I grow older and look back at a very non-linear trajectory of my work and career that doesn't necessarily fit the mold of where I should have been or how it should have been done, I have been rethinking the definition of success. The closest I can come to is the following: Success is a constant journey of learning and growing and pushing oneself further. It is that feeling of excitement about what you do and living a life you can feel proud of as you look back.

LEADERSHIP

What does this mean for you?

Dr. King was not victorious in every organizing effort. He often made choices to accommodate opponents. He sometimes cut deals when he thought the best outcome was not possible. He infuriated ideological purists who felt that he too frequently compromised. Certainly, President Obama has not achieved all of his policy goals. He too has angered many who felt that he is too frequently conciliatory. But despite their failures, our experts perceive both King and Obama as worthy of the highest ratings as leaders.

Leadership is a process of social influence, which maximizes the efforts of others, towards the achievement of a goal.

Someone who empowers others/anything.

Who/what represents a leader/philosophy you follow?

Nobel Laureate Professor Muhammad Yunus, founder of Grameen Bank and a global leader in the fight against poverty.

John Ridley

Writer, Director, Producer; Founder And CEO, NŌ Studios

BACKGROUND

Who are you and what helped make you who you are?

Business-wise, other than writing and producing, I started a collaborative workspace arts hub in Milwaukee, called NŌ Studios. "NŌ," with an elongation over the "O," is a Japanese word that means art, skill or talent. I thought it was ironic that we hear "No" so often in life, and I wanted to turn a negative into a positive.

Describing who I am is the hard part, so I will start with the second part of the question, "What helped make you who you are." I credit my parents and a long line of teachers who helped shape me in ways that I didn't understand when I was in school. I credit the people who gave me opportunities, not just to succeed, but to fail. I think the big thing is not to just say, "Okay they failed" and move on, but see where their strengths are, help them understand their strengths and weaknesses, and encourage them to lean to their strengths. I certainly had that on my journey to *wherever* it is I am right now. So, a long line of people helped shape me, but certainly my parents, teachers, bosses or leaders, who have given me jobs.

I also think it's one thing to give somebody a job and review them saying, "Okay, you're doing well or you're not doing well," but people who give you a job should also guide and mentor you. I was fortunate, I was able to work with several different bosses, typically show runners, who could manage many personalities. As I look back at my pluses and minuses, I think I was talented, but I was headstrong, which is not always a great thing. When you're young it's good to have energy and enthusiasm, but it's not good if you are unaware of your weaknesses or your failings. I think I had some good bosses who were able to compartmentalize my strengths and my weaknesses and help me build on the things that I was doing well and tolerate some of the things I wasn't doing well. They gave me an opportunity to grow, not in the 1950s movies, "Son, I see great things for you" manner, but saw that I was a very good employee. I was a self-starter. If I was given an assignment, I got it done. I never missed deadlines, and I still don't today. I do the work, I do it thoroughly, and I go above and beyond in terms of the work that's in front of me.

In my profession it's not just about getting the job done, for example, writing a script that's 60 pages. There's more to it than putting words on paper. Does it have some humor? Does it have heart? Does it have rhythms? You don't want every scene to be exactly three pages long and start the same way and end the same way. What are the things that would make a disparate audience laugh or cry or think? I say these things with a bit of perspective, I don't want it to come off like I was a genius, but others saw me as someone who would get the work done on time, who would not come in with excuses.

I did everything that I needed to do to be a good partner and a good employee in the Writer's Room. To be successful, you have to learn to work with people with different personalities, but you also have to be able to go off and write a script, do what you need to do, get it in and make it sing. People knew that when my script came in, it was going to be a cut above. That's not just natural talent. Just like any job, any profession, you must understand what makes *the cut above*, then you have to work hard so that you can deliver. When you deliver consistently, people notice. I loved what I was doing, and I knew, frankly, as a person of color, that I needed to work twice as hard and twice as long to get half as much. My parents prepared me and my sisters for this reality, so when I started working in the early 90s I was prepared.

How did you get started?

People recognized they needed to have more people of color in television. In the days of Sanford and Son, you may have had people of color in front of the camera, but it was largely a white writer's room with white producers. So, I came in during a time when people realized they needed to open things up a bit. I think the expectations where, "We're opening this up, but we don't expect much. We'll see what they can do." So, my thing was, "If you let me in, you may not expect much, but you're going to get a lot, and if you expect a lot, you're going to get even more." It's still the way for me.

I came out to Los Angeles in the 90s and at that time, relatively speaking, there was an explosion of shows. Fox was a relatively new network. When I came out it was about 10-years old, but they hadn't had much traction. But then they started putting on shows with people of color; In Living Color, Martin, and Living Single. Back then UPN was new, the UPN is now the CW, but at that time they were trying to figure out how to build an audience and their thing was, programming for people of color. They called that type of programming, "Urban." The "Urban Market," as if black people only lived in cities. I was like, "Why don't you just say black people?" But that was what they called it, "Urban." It was tough because I did not grow up in an urban environment, and everything had to be very hip hop, *NWA* and stuff like that. My perspective was, "Hold on one second, there's a lot of us and we are not all the same." So, I would try to get in a joke about James Baldwin or Ralph Ellison, maybe not that arcane, but it didn't fly. There was still this monolithic sense of what *Blackness* meant. But I was in, I was working and that's how it started.

I was a trainee on a show on NBC, a very short-lived show. Then my second show was the Martin Show, which was a big deal because I met my wife on that show. I was trying to make everything an opportunity while not trying to be *opportunistic*. But everything was an opportunity, and it started with just wanting to get my script in. Let me learn, let me have a chance to show myself. Everything, every interaction was of value, that was very important to me.

I think writers are at the low end of the totem pole, especially black writers, and back in the day, younger writers were way down at the bottom. Things would happen, and I would wonder, "Am I being disrespected because I'm a writer or am I being disrespected because I'm a *Black* writer?" And in those disrespects, "How do I respond?" If you're being disrespected as a writer, sometimes you take it, but sometimes you have to stand up for yourself. I think that was the lesson I learned as I grew older and had more access, authority, and responsibility. If you really have a sense of self and intestinal fortitude, then you should be reaching a hand back and pulling people along, not shoving a hand in people's face who are (hopefully) the people you are going to inspire and educate and learn from and help to bring along. So, for me, the journey was moving from the Martin Show, to Fresh Prince, and then The John Larroquette Show, which was a big deal because that was a show with a white lead and an ethnically mixed cast. At that time, it was a big deal to move from a predominately black show and demonstrate, "I can write anything."

People of Color were such a new entity at that time, that we were like anything else that was new, easy to disregard. People were overt, but not hardcore. No one was waving confederate flags when we were driving to work in the morning. It's what people now call privilege. There is a lot of "bumper-stickerism" going on, people use phrases like, "Privilege" or "Woke," etc. I don't mean to diminish the meaning, but sometimes I think we take the struggle and we reduce it to a catchphrase. This bothers me because our struggle is more nuanced than that. So sometimes I don't call it privilege, I call it myopic, and that's because that's the way some people have lived.

Even today, there are still people who say, "Yeah, okay, you can write black stuff, but how can you write stuff with white people?" That's weird to me. As a person of color, which I believe is also similar for women, and anyone considered "the other," we live in many worlds; it's like being bilingual or trilingual. We can speak the language of the prevailing culture, but the prevailing culture can't speak our language because they don't live in our world. So, it's always weird to me when people are surprised that I wrote U-Turn. I remember going into a meeting after the film came out with an executive who said, "Oh wow, I couldn't believe that you wrote U-Turn because it was Sean Penn, it was Nick Nolte, and I just thought it would be a white guy who came in." He was stunned. That's the world we live in every day. If you're a young Latina girl, you live in three or four worlds. But they would never assume that you could write Game of Thrones. Why not?

Even now in 2019, in so many places it's still a risk to hire a woman or a person of color. The adage *working twice as long and twice as hard to get half as much* is still true. I don't think that I'm here by accident. I think I'm an okay writer, I think I'm okay at the things I did, but I think more than anything, that my parents taught me, when you walk into that room, people may assume that you're not capable, but it doesn't matter what they think - it matters how you think about yourself and how you respond to that belief in yourself.

SUCCESS

Define Success.

This might sound trite, but to me, success is based on the days that you're "You," when you're happy that you're you. I feel successful on the days where I get to go to my son's basketball game at 3:00 PM and I'm one of only a couple of dads there. Success is when you have a parent who's ill and you can afford to make sure they have good medical care; that makes me happy. Honestly, if there is any other thing you're looking for from success - if you are focused on money or stature - those things come and go, but the trips I've taken with my family or when they've come to visit me on set and Orlando Bloom tells your son, "Oh my God, look at how handsome you are. You're going to be a heartbreaker." That makes me happy. Honestly, being able to do that is what's important.

I don't have a catchphrase for success, but one of the things that's very important to me is that the sets I work on are positive work environments. Every weekend films open, they may be the best film ever made, and an audience doesn't show up. There may be a crappy film, and everybody goes to see it. You don't know what's going to happen, and it's hard to make it all work. So, what you've got to do, in my opinion, is at least have a work environment where people are energized every day, where they are appreciated because of their skillset, where they are encouraged to do their best work, and if nothing else, people come out of it and say, "Oh my God, this was fun and it was creative and we got to do things that we just never do on any other show in any other space." That makes me happy.

I can't control how the audience is going to receive my work, but what I can control is people's experiences on the set every single day - whether they're a PA or whether they're an executive visiting the set, everybody feels that they're treated equally and fairly and that they have value - because they do.

When you engage with people and let them know that what they do is important, they show up and do their best work. That's how I'd like to be treated and that's how I think people deserve to be treated, and that is how I gauge success.

What was your greatest business challenge?

My biggest challenge is that I really like to multitask; I love to work. The most important things to me are my family and my work. I love to write, so part of my biggest business challenge is when I go to my bosses while I'm working on a project and say, "Okay, what else you got?" And they say, "Well, you're doing something." "Yeah, I know, but I'm turning that in tomorrow and then I'm going to have a week to sit around not doing anything, I'm going to freak out."

I'll hand in the spec script and they say, "When did you write this?" I'll say, "What do you mean when did I write it? We were off at Christmas for two weeks and here's a script…" I'm sometimes judged by peoples' limitations on how much they think I should do. But until I mess-up and the quality of what I write suffers, I'm going to keep doing what I do.

LEADERSHIP

What does this mean for you?

I think leadership would be representing the kind of person that inspires others. There are times when you must be tough, there are times you must make hard decisions, there are times you must do things that are unpleasant, but in those different times, are you inspiring people?

The thing that makes me most happy is when people come up to me and say, "I would follow you anywhere. I will work with you again any time." In an industry where directors are known for being ogres, just mean, nasty people, I really appreciate when people say, "Oh my God, this was the quietest set I've ever worked on…" The people you bring along by being accessible and inspiring them really matters. It drives loyalty, and loyalty means everything to me. I'm loyal to my people. I demonstrate that I will protect them and have their back. Listen more than you speak, let your employees know that you don't know everything and that they were hired because they are experts at what they do, that is leadership.

Who/what represents a leader/philosophy you follow?

Respect the people you work with and let everyone know that they're valued. Be patient and engaged.

If you respect me, I will respect you. It's really that more than anything else. I want to be respected, I've earned the right to be respected, but I never earn the right to disrespect people.

I was on a set and there was a PA, a young guy, I walked by him and said, "How you doing? How's everything? Good to see you." Just that, not anything more than that, and one day he said, "You know, everybody here loves working with you because you talk to us and most of the time directors will just walk by you." Maybe there's a time when something is happening on the set and I'm lost in my head, and I'm just walking around trying to clear my mind. But I still say hello. It's not that I feel good about saying hello, I feel bad that saying hello suddenly moves you up five spots on the rostrum because most people don't. It stuns me how many people are fine not putting in the work to just be nice.

There are times where people confuse niceness with weakness, but there's a saying I read years ago in high school and it goes roughly, "Treat your enemies as your friends because if you do that, you can avoid conflict. But if conflict comes, you can go to war without guilt."

STRUGGLE

Define struggle.

My father was a doctor, my mother was a teacher, and we grew up with a nice middle-class lifestyle. I had a good education, a wonderful wife, I have good friends. So, comparatively speaking how much struggle was there, I mean, I had every advantage in the world.

I was never quite sure how I'd get from there to where I am now, but I also never doubted that I would get here. It was never going to be any other way because I was going to do what I needed to do and that goes back to the *twice as hard, twice as long*, perspective. It goes back to doing the work. There are people out there who are more talented than me, who are brighter than me, and maybe the opportunity never showed up for them. But there are also people who are not more talented than me, and are doing way more than I am. So sometimes it balances out. Part of what I want to do now with the end game of my life, is to make sure that people who do have talent get their shot. That's why we set up NŌ Studios in Milwaukee, that's why I do as much as I can with the Academy of Motion Picture Arts and Sciences. Being a member of the Academy is wonderful, but what makes it wonderful is being able to advocate for women and people of color.

When I came out to California, I knew it was going to be tough and hard. That's all I needed to know. I didn't need to complain about it, I didn't need to hear about it, I knew it was going to be tough; it's tough all over. It's tough in every industry for people of color, for women, for those who are traditionally disenfranchised. So, my thing was, I was not going to complain. Once you make that bargain to get in, it's too late to go, "Oh Jesus." There are times I commiserate with other people and there are times when I shake my head and say, "This person got that?" And clearly what did they have going for them? I can tell you, the whiteness of their skin and the meat between their legs. You can complain or you can prevail, so my thing was, I'm going to prevail.

DIVERSITY

Define this in your own terms.

I try to get people to stop using the word diversity now because I think diversity was something we wanted to achieve in the 70s, "Hey, let's get <u>one</u> woman in this office, let's get <u>one</u> black guy in here." Technically straight white men are in the minority in this country. So, if we're going to talk about diversity, we would need to talk about getting one straight white man into this environment versus how to get one black woman in here. So, I like to say "Reflective." Is our writing room reflective of the world? Is our show reflective? Because when you start saying reflective, then it changes the conversation because if we are reflective, most people should be women, Hispanic, Black, etc.

If we are really holding a mirror to society, then what we see is going to be a whole lot different. I just feel like working towards *diversity* still implies one of these, one from column "A," one from column "B," and that don't get it done.

How have you managed this?

I practice what I preach. I go into my writer's rooms and most people in critical decision-making positions are people of color. On the series American Crime, 90% of our directors were women, people of color, and people of orientations other than my own. That's not an accident. So, my thing is to be intentional in providing opportunities for women and people of color and be a catalyst for change. One of those directors on American Crime, Nicole Kassell, is directing Watchmen on HBO. Rachel Morrison, one of our directors, was the DP on Black Panther and she's Oscar nominated. Vic Mahoney is working on Star Wars. They all would have succeeded without me, but it makes me feel good that we were a position to help them along the way.

LEGACY

What do you want to leave behind for others, what is your legacy?

I would love my legacy to be that you can work on a film or TV, in very intense environments, but you can be respectful of people and their time. I don't spend a lot of time in the writer's room, they come in, we talk about what needs to be talked about. If you're an adult, then you can go off to your office, or you can go home, or you can go to the beach, I don't care where you go if you do your work. And then bring it back in and let's get cracking. Respect, dignity, positive work environment, the opposite of everything that's Hollywood.

For example, there was a colorist by the name of Beau that I worked with. He did the first episode of American Crime and it was so good that I called to thank him. He wasn't in so I left a message. I said, "Will you have Beau give me a call when he has a minute?" And his agent called back and he said, "Why are you calling Beau?" And I said, "I wanted to thank him, I thought he did an amazing job, it was great." And he said, "Okay, well I'll pass it along." I really wanted to talk to him, but okay. Beau called me back and he said, "I'm really sorry I had my agent call. I didn't know why you were calling, nobody's ever called to thank me before."

A lot of the people I work with now are in their 20s and 30s. My career could end tomorrow, that's the reality in Hollywood, you're as good as your last project. So, I may be done, but the philosophy that I put in place will live on.

The people that are going out there now, are going to be working for many years to come and they are going to take my philosophy, how I approach the work, and carry it forward.

Why is this important for you?

My philosophy is not simply about work, I think it's about how we engage life in general. The #Me Too movement is indicative of how men in power, or powerful men, or aggressive men abuse their power. So, to me, it's in business as in life, in sports as in life, as in family as in life, treat people how you'd want to be treated.

There was a study done on toxic masculinity addressing how men are raised to be tough and emotionless. A big part of growth and change is getting over the sense of that's what leadership looks like. That's what being a general is - no thought, no feeling, do your job, you have to, you're a man. Go out there, climb that mountain, slay the dragons, go home, if you lost 100 men in the battle, don't cry. Show no emotion and go fight another day. That was probably great in the 50s, that ain't the world today.

QUOTE OR WORDS TO LIVE BY/ADVICE

I try to eschew clichés and bumper sticker catchphrases, they always annoy me as a writer, I mean honestly. At the same time, I feel like I have given you many of them. So, I will say this, just know yourself. Know how you feel in your most private moments, be honest with yourself, and you'll be fine. There will be times when you feel like you don't know anything, and you have to go and stand in front of people and pretend you know everything, and there will be times when you know a lot but will have to back off and not overwhelm people with your intellect. And then there are times where you just got to be yourself and if people can deal with that, great.

For example, I had a situation on a show where I wasn't show running, I wasn't in charge, I was a director. I said to the producers, "It's very important for you to know that I'm not a yeller or a screamer." The producer's response was, "Yeah, yeah, yeah, okay, we get it, we get it." And I said, "It's very important for you to understand that." And there came a moment where they called me into the office very upset because they didn't feel like I was taking charge. The producer started yelling, and I said, "I got to stop you because when I took this job, I told you I'm not a yeller and a screamer and I said I don't respond to yelling and screaming. So, if you can't modulate your tone, I'm getting up and walking out and that's the last conversation we'll have."

The calmness and the surety in my voice changed everything. I had a moment where I understood, as James Baldwin would say, "I'm not your Negro." This wasn't a racial thing, but in that moment, everything changed because I didn't need them, they do not own me, and they do not own my style, I'm coming in, I'm the gentle guy, if that doesn't work for you, there is nothing about this job that I need because I would rather be with my kids or I would rather be with my wife.

Some people believe that yelling and being a monster is power. Power is having control over your own life and your own circumstances and when you present that kind of power to people, they don't know what to do. That's why Oprah is powerful, that's why Beyoncé is powerful, that's why Obama is powerful. That's why the students at Marjory Stoneman Douglas High School are powerful. The students made their voices heard, they owned their power, and people tried to shut them down. You can't shut them down. People are trying to rein in Alexandria Cortez Ocasio, they can't. Don't even try and rein that young lady in, she's going to be her, she's 30 years old, she's a socialist, she's a rock star. You better learn how to just step aside.

There is a generation coming who has been through everything; they crossed the border because they believe in their dream. So power is when you know yourself, when nobody can control you and you don't have to get angry. That to me is success, and leadership, and legacy all rolled up into one.

Ida Shum, Esq.

AI/AR Strategy & Open Innovation Leader, Samsung.

BACKGROUND

Who are you and what helped make you who you are?

Reformed Patent Attorney. I am Ida Shum, and I have been fortunate to have the love and support of my great family, friends, and colleagues.

How did you get started?

My first job was working in a lab at Cal State Los Angeles, with my Mother's adviser, Thomas Onak. He focused on boron chemistry.

SUCCESS

Define Success.

Being able to do what you love and enjoy. It's the feeling of not 'working' but doing something on your own terms.

What was your greatest business challenge?

Knowing when to bite your tongue. We all feel passionate about projects or initiatives at work. However, management may not see eye to eye with you and your ideas may get pushed aside. Even when you know your idea is better, more efficient, and effective, it's tempting to provide evidence as to why your approach is the way to go. But sometimes it is smarter to wait than to be insubordinate or uncooperative.

What's your business philosophy?

Conduct yourself in such a way that if someone spoke badly of you, no one would believe it. Your reputation is your greatest asset and you should protect it.

LEADERSHIP

What does this mean for you? Can you define it in a sentence?

A leader is not someone who leads, but someone others want to follow.

Who represents a leader/philosophy you follow?

Aside from my mom, dad, and grandmother, it would be Nelson Mandela. All share the traits of perseverance, with the ability to balance integrity, confidence, and hard work. To have faith in their beliefs and not sit around waiting. You have to be proactive and use your voice to enact positive change.

STRUGGLE

Define struggle.

It's more what it isn't... Just because you're struggling, does not mean you're failing. My Dad would always remind me not to give up.

What have your struggles been and how have you worked through or overcome the struggles?

I'm struggling to balance my family, work, and enough downtime for myself. It's important to take a step back and not over-think. That will just stress you out!

DIVERSITY

Define this in your own terms.

Difference of thought, culture, geography, and perspective to create a holistic view.

How have you managed this?

Creating an environment that enables one to be comfortable enough to express ideas openly and freely. This requires commitment and action to build a safe space.

LEGACY

What do you want to leave behind for others, what is your legacy?

It sounds trite, but I would like to be remembered for positive contributions to society and my community.

Why is this important for you?

It's the hope that the world is a better place for my daughter and future generations.

QUOTE OR WORDS TO LIVE BY/ADVICE

Do what you enjoy and enjoy your life!

Tina Zee

Project Manager, Nestlé USA.

BACKGROUND

Who are you and what helped make you who you are?

I am a contributor and a connector. That is what first comes to mind; however, that is the role I've played throughout the years with family, friends, in business and my community. They have been the common thread in what I DO. But who I AM, while in those roles are: Compassion, Love, Generosity, Loyal, and Power.

My years as a youth laid the foundation for who I am. I was very fortunate and grew up in a loving family and was never in lack of anything I needed. All of my basic needs were provided for and then some, lots! Although my parents were divorced, it wasn't traumatic for me because I didn't know them any other way. They made sure we were always together as a family throughout the year, not just holidays. Growing up in the diverse cities of Chicago and Honolulu, I was exposed to a variety of cultures, food, traditions, religions, and lifestyles. Different was normal.

As an adult, I've had challenges that were definitely life changing and helped confirm who I am. When challenges arise, you always have a choice, to sink or swim. There were times I wanted to sink, but I chose to swim, with a life jacket. My life jacket is made of personal development workshops, self-help books, volunteerism, family, friends, my life coach Andrea Quinn, "Campowerment" events, and a strong commitment to myself.

I was very fortunate to have been provided with so many opportunities growing up and as an adult. It is important to me, to pay it forward and help others. I have volunteered for many years with various organizations, mainly youth oriented. Through the years, I have been a member of various business associations, non-profit boards, and committees. When I'm serving as a mentor or connecting people to resources, it is fulfilling. My desire is to help bring peace, happiness, and success to people, in whatever form that may be for them.

I have had a variety of careers, yet who I am has been consistent throughout. I've been a corporate meeting and event planner, volunteer director, entrepreneur, training coordinator, fundraising and development manager, marketing manager, and project manager. However, I am not defined by my title or position. When I show up as my I AMs, I always succeed.

How did you get started?

Oh my. As you can tell by the number of positions I just listed, I feel as though I've tried everything! Constantly on the search for the answer to the timeless question "What do you want to be when you grow up?" I started with the basics, education. After I received my master's degree in Sport & Leisure Service Management, I worked in sports for a hot minute and then reality hit me in the wallet! Sallie Mae. Who is Sallie Mae? Oh yeah, that small financial institution that wanted their money back for my undergraduate student loans. My job in sports wasn't paying enough for Sallie, so I entered Corporate America! And then it just became the continuous search for a fulfilling career. Networking played a big part in my career history. I wish it was taught in high school. How to work a room full of people you don't know. How to build rapport and maintain a professional relationship. Who you know can open doors. What you know can seal the deal. They're both important.

SUCCESS

Define Success.

Success is learning and achieving. Giving your all so regardless of the outcome, you know you gave it your best, learned from the experience and that you were grateful for the opportunity.

What was your greatest business challenge?

My greatest business challenge was launching and maintaining our family beverage business, Tibetan Tea, Inc. The product was a ready-to-drink, lightly carbonated, natural-energy tea beverage. I ran the company for six years and wore every hat … marketing, packaging, operations, finance, shipping, distribution, sales, administrative. You name it, I did it. My father was the beverage guru and was running his other beverage company at the same time. It was a new industry for me to learn and my entire life was about the business. I learned about many things I never could have imagined. Pallet configurations … plastic versus wood? Does it really matter? Yes, it did!

It was a life changing experience and I'm grateful for the opportunity. There were definite highs and lows and in between. I encountered many challenges running the business itself and trying to compete in such a saturated market against companies with deep pockets and a lot of employee resources. However, the greatest challenge was the effect it had on my relationship with my father. Family businesses have a completely different set of complexities. Not only did I acquire a wealth of business knowledge, I learned a great deal about myself. Even though we ended up selling the company, it was definitely a success.

What is your business philosophy?

My business philosophy is the same philosophy I have for life. I am not perfect, but I try to think about the impact of my actions, on other people, animals, and the environment. Business with a conscience. Take care of the people you employ. When you truly take care of them, you're taking care of their families and communities and the positive energy has an impact greater than one can imagine.

LEADERSHIP

What does this mean for you? Can you define it in a sentence?

There is a poem by Stephen Grellet, that I have hanging in my apartment, that sums up leadership for me:

> "I expect to pass through this world but once; any good thing therefore that I can do, or any kindness that I can show to a fellow creature, let me do it now. Let me not defer or neglect it, for I shall not pass this way again."

Who/what represents a leader/philosophy you follow?

My Auntie Linda is a true leader. She lives her life and manages her company with a conscience. I have always known her to genuinely care for the well-being of other people and animals and assist in any way she can. She doesn't do anything for the recognition; she actually prefers none. My grandmother passed before I was born, but my father always says: Auntie Linda is just like my grandmother. She is trusted, admired, and well-respected by many.

STRUGGLE

Define struggle.

To struggle is to work with resistance. Applying effort to achieve something that seems unattainable.

What have your struggles been and how have you worked through or overcome the struggle?

I have had an internal struggle with myself for most of my adult life. I always admired people who knew what they wanted to be when they grew up and just followed the breadcrumb path to get there. When I was in elementary school, I thought my path was high school, college, graduate school, and successful business woman. Everything happened except the successful business woman part because in my mind, that was supposed to happen immediately after graduate school. So maybe that was a little unrealistic. Year after year passed and I wasn't where I thought I should be in my life. I was on a journey to find my purpose and passion. I worked in various industries and was successful in my roles, but still didn't feel the connection to my purpose, my contribution to the greater good. When I started volunteering, I began to find my purpose and passion. Most of the organizations and projects were youth- and women-focused. I served as a disaster relief volunteer with the Red Cross in Mississippi after Hurricane Katrina and saw the positive impact of my time and dedication and that felt great. I was a founding member of a non-profit and served on Boards and Committees. However, the internal struggle didn't completely end. And then I started exploring meditation and mindfulness practices and that opened a whole new world for me. And it helped me realize that I've been on the right path. So, if breadcrumbs had been thrown down, I would have missed many key experiences and I wouldn't have as much appreciation for where I am and who I am today. Perhaps it isn't a struggle anymore, but a constant conscious state of growing, learning, and reinventing myself.

DIVERSITY

Define this in your own terms.

Diversity is an all-encompassing representation that recognizes all people and everything that makes them who they are as individuals.

How have you managed this?

I am ethnically diverse. I grew up in Chicago, Illinois and Honolulu, Hawaii. Both cities exude diversity, so it was my norm. It wasn't until I attended Bowling Green State University, in Ohio, that I realized I was different. I remember my father flew in the day before me from a business trip and was going to help me get settled. He picked me up at the Toledo Airport and told me it was going to be a very different place for me. He was right. It wasn't a bad experience, except for the weather, but it was eye opening and made me appreciate my diverse background. I was also a sports management major, so I was the minority again as most students in my classes were men. After Bowling Green, I lived in Atlanta, Las Vegas, and Los Angeles; all diverse cities. Because of my background and experiences, I've always been open-minded and welcomed diversity. Life would be boring without it.

LEGACY

What do you want to leave behind for others, what is your legacy?

Often as a volunteer, you never know the full impact you had on someone. I can only hope that I made a positive contribution and because of that, another positive contribution was made, and so on.

Why is this important for you?

There is so much pain and suffering in the world. I'd like to be remembered for helping people find peace, happiness, and success in their lives. I was blessed with a gift, and as long as I am on this earth, receiving all it has to offer, it is my responsibility and honor to give back.

QUOTE OR WORDS TO LIVE BY/ADVICE

The only thing you have control over, is yourself ... your thoughts, perceptions, actions, words, beliefs ... choose them carefully and with a conscience.

I am what time, circumstance, history, have made of me, certainly, but I am also, much more than that. So are we all. – James A. Baldwin

ACKNOWLEDGMENTS

I have always been impressed by people with the ability to connect with their audience and inspire positive action. My father was a pastor and an entrepreneur, I watched him influence others using the power of words. My mother was a homemaker and our rock; supportive and protective of her family and dedicated to instilling in her children a will to thrive, not just survive, in a world that was not always welcoming. Their ability to galvanize support and compel people to action was a force of will that transformed the lives of those around them.

As I grew older, I learned that this phenomenon was called leadership, the power or ability to lead other people.[cxxxviii] I have seen many examples of people in positions of leadership who do not have the respect, authority, or gravitas to be effective. They are leaders in title only.

A *despot*, a *boss*, an *owner*, a *ruler*, and those born into positions of power may have the *title* of leader and the responsibility of leadership but may not have the skills to lead. Many individuals put forward as leaders were in positions of power, but did not demonstrate the caring, dedication, and integrity of the people who inspired me.

I began to understand that with power comes responsibility, not as a catchphrase or a slogan, but as a value demonstrated by behaviors, and my definition of leadership evolved into, "the ability to effectively and responsibly engage with people, processes, and programs, to achieve organizational, team, or individual goals."

Leadership is more than title, charm, or charisma. True leaders demonstrate ability, effectiveness, responsibility, engagement, and goal achievement, while communicating effectively and acting with integrity.

My mother encouraged us to read, everything from comic books to history books. My father believed that experience was critical to growth and was influential in my decision to join the Peace Corps.

I became a student of the world and gained perspective and experience from the best *and* worst examples of leadership. As a Peace Corps Volunteer in Honduras, I listened to the children and women of the communities where I lived and worked and gained wisdom. As an executive and consultant, I learned the pitfalls of ego and arrogance. I saw the failures of those who surrounded themselves with sycophants and witnessed the success of those interested in honesty and truth.

We have experiences in our lives that can be transformative, if we are able to learn from those experiences and apply the lessons appropriately. We can learn from the good and the bad if we are willing to engage the world with a sense of wonder.

I read, and listened, and engaged with others and found inspiration in the writings of Toni Morrison, Howard Zinn, Lerone Bennett, Jr., Gabriel García Márquez, Cornel West, Harvey Mackay, Bell Hooks, Ronald Takaki, Michael Josephson, Ellis Cose, Zora Neale Hurston, James Baldwin, and many others. There were five books essential to my development in the areas of leadership, accountability, and positive action:

- The Servant: A Simple Story About Leadership, by James C. Hunter.
- QBQ!® The Question Behind the Question, by John G. Miller.
- The Oz Principle: Getting Results Through Individual and Organizational Accountability, by Roger Connors, Tom Smith, and Craig Hickman.
- The Thin Book of Naming Elephants: How to Surface Undiscussables for Greater Organizational Success, by Sue Annis Hammond and Andrea B. Mayfield.
- Execution, by Larry Bossidy and Ram Charan.

These books, along with life experiences, education, and training, provided a framework for understanding the roles, responsibilities, expectations, and challenges of leadership.

I am thankful to all those who took the time to mentor me and share their wisdom.

My heartfelt gratitude and appreciation go out to Analisa Davis, for your time and edits, and to my Chief Editor, Niloufer Pabla. Your reviews, revisions, encouragement, and unlimited patience were appreciated more than you could have imagined. Thank You!

INDEX

15 percent rule, 126
5-Core Skills Of Exceptional Leaders, 32
A need, 29
A want, 29
A.D.V.I.C.E., 97
Ability, 23
Accountability, 25, 73, 97, 99, 106, 123
Adaptation, 41
Advice, 97
Appreciative Inquiry, 35
Appropriate skill, 26
Assurance, 40, 41
Authority, 30
Behavior, 71, 72, 76
Behavior Breeds Behavior, 71, 76
behaviors, 7, 19, 22, 26, 30, 33, 37, 38, 53, 56, 57, 63, 71, 72, 73, 86, 98, 104, 105, 106, 108, 109, 117, 122, 139, 143, 144, 213
Business Model innovation, 43
C.A.R.E.S. Model, 25, 26
C.H.O.I.C.E.S., 111, 112, 113
CARI(ng)® Process, 26
Characteristics Of Trustworthiness, 88
Clear expectations, 26
Commitment, 31, 111, 112, 114, 115
communication, 7, 8, 19, 25, 35, 36, 53, 54, 55, 56, 57, 58, 59, 61, 62, 73, 75, 80, 86, 98, 101, 112, 116, 126, 127, 130, 140, 141
Communication, 25, 35, 36, 53, 55, 56, 57, 59, 60, 98, 99, 112, 218
conflict, 133, 136, 139, 140, 141, 142, 157
Continuous Learning, 35, 36
Cultivating Genuineness, 35, 37
Dialogue, 36, 61, 62, 63, 65, 66
effective communication, 53
Effectiveness, 23
elephant in the room, 78
Emotional Intelligence, 35, 37
Empathy, 40, 41
Engagement, 23, 26, 36, 112
Facilitation, 62, 67, 70
fear, 33, 36, 74, 93, 120, 121, 130, 137, 145, 146, 182
Fear, 118, 145
five (5) qualities of leadership, 23
Goal Achievement, 23
hope, 93, 94, 95, 110, 133, 138, 158, 177, 181, 184, 212
hot buttons, 56, 57, 58, 59, 60
Hot Buttons, 56, 59
I.T.E.M., 122
Incentives, 26
Innovation, 38, 39, 41, 42, 44
Integrity, 38, 39, 44, 45, 46, 47, 48, 50, 97, 98, 99
leader, 20, 22, 25, 26, 28, 29, 32, 33, 34, 35, 54, 70, 73, 87, 97, 98, 101, 106, 132, 135, 143, 146, 156, 162, 167, 172, 175, 176, 180, 186, 190, 194, 200, 210, 213
Leaders, 22, 25, 26, 27, 38, 39, 55, 64, 85, 86, 89, 91, 93, 94, 95, 97, 100, 104, 108, 110, 111, 112, 114, 116, 118, 120, 121, 123, 126, 132, 134, 136, 139, 143, 147, 149, 153, 162

leadership, 19
Leadership, 3, 9, 19, 20, 22, 23, 24, 28, 29, 30, 33, 36, 38, 39, 44, 82, 145, 156, 180, 218
Manage, 30, 116, 117
Marketing innovation, 43
MBWA, 126
Nine (9) Skills for Facilitation©, 67
Organizational innovation, 43
Patience, 33, 34, 71, 145
Perseverance, 148
Perspective, 108, 148
Philosophy, 32
Power, 30, 71, 112, 145, 208
Practice, 33, 34, 144, 145, 166
Process innovation, 43
Product innovation, 43
QBQ!®, 73, 74, 75, 214
R.A.I.S.E., 106, 107
relationships, 20, 26, 29, 34, 37, 57, 71, 82, 86, 87, 109, 114, 116, 117, 122, 139, 140, 141, 179, 185, 189
Relationships, 116
Reliability, 40, 41
Responsibility, 25, 105, 112
Responsiveness, 40, 41
Reward, 26, 87, 127
servant leadership, 28, 29
Servant Leadership, 28, 31

Service, 26, 38, 39, 40, 41, 112, 209
Skill, 26, 32, 45, 67
SPF, 126, 128
Style, 32, 218
success, 19
Success, 20
Successful Continuous Development, 33, 35, 36
Supervision, 24, 218
Tangibles, 40, 41
TDC Communication Exercise, 56, 57, 59
The Oz Principle®, 37
The Servant, 28, 29, 30, 218
Trait, 32, 218
trust, 22, 40, 48, 50, 55, 56, 57, 59, 85, 86, 87, 111, 115, 124, 131, 162, 182, 183, 184
Trustworthy, 85
Understanding of others, 33, 34
Understanding of self, 33, 34
Understanding of the objective, 33, 34
values, 7, 19, 20, 22, 25, 26, 28, 30, 32, 33, 35, 37, 38, 45, 63, 86, 87, 88, 89, 90, 98, 105, 111, 115, 120, 140, 148, 149, 176, 179, 183, 185, 186, 187
Values, 98

ENDNOTES

[i] The Death of responsibility. https://www.linkedin.com/pulse/death-responsibility-russell-davis-sphr-shrm-scp/
[ii] http://www.stopstreetharassment.org/wp-content/uploads/2018/01/Full-Report-2018-National-Study-on-Sexual-Harassment-and-Assault.pdf
[iii] Definition of Leadership. http://www.merriam-webster.com/dictionary/leadership
[iv] Definition of Success. http://www.merriam-webster.com/dictionary/success
[v] https://psychcentral.com/blog/what-self-care-is-and-what-it-isnt-2/
[vi] Supervision. http://managementhelp.org/blogs/supervision/about/
[vii] Interpretation of Leader: PAKISTAN PLANNING AND MANAGEMENT INSTITUTE. LEADERSHIP IN PROJECT MANAGEMENT. SYED ANWAR-UL-HASAN BOKHARI ACTING GENERAL MANAGER CIVIL SERVICE REFORM UNIT. FEBRUARY 24, 2005. WHAT IS LEADERSHIP?. http://www.slideserve.com/jaden/leadership-in-project-management
[viii] Leading Learning Today, Leading Tomorrow, Unit I: Personal Leadership Skills; 3. Understanding Your Leadership Style, p. 2 http://extension.psu.edu/publications/ua416, The Pennsylvania State University, 328 Boucke Building, University Park, PA 16802-5901. Produced by Information and Communication Technologies in the College of Agricultural Sciences © The Pennsylvania State University 2005 CAT UA416, 3M10/05ps4719
[ix] BusinessDictionary.com. http://www.businessdictionary.com/definition/servant-leadership.html
[x] Servant Leadership; GreenLeaf.org. https://www.greenleaf.org/what-is-servant-leadership/
[xi] The Servant: A Simple Story About the True Essence of Leadership Sep 1, 1998, by James C. Hunter, Prima Publishing, p. 28
[xii] Ibid., p. 40
[xiii] Ibid., p. 41
[xiv] Ibid., p. 67
[xv] Ibid., p. 88
[xvi] Ibid., p. 89
[xvii] Ibid., p. 166
[xviii] Ibid., p. 124
[xix] Ibid., p. 167
[xx] http://www.merriam-webster.com/dictionary/manage
[xxi] James C. Hunter, "The Servant: A Simple Story About the True Essence of Leadership," 1998, Prima Publishing, p. 28
[xxii] Ibid., p. 30
[xxiii] Ibid., p. 30
[xxiv] Definition of style. http://www.merriam-webster.com/dictionary/style
[xxv] Definition of Trait: http://www.merriam-webster.com/dictionary/trait

[xxvi] Definition of philosophy. http://www.merriam-webster.com/dictionary/philosophy
[xxvii] Definition of skill. http://www.thefreedictionary.com/skill
[xxviii] Cooperrider, D.L. and Whitney, D., "Appreciative Inquiry: A positive revolution in change." In P. Holman and T. Devane (eds.), The Change Handbook, Berrett-Koehler Publishers, Inc., pp. 245–263
[xxix] Definition of emotional intelligence; http://www.oxforddictionaries.com/us/definition/american_english/emotional-intelligence
[xxx] Definition of intelligence; https://en.wikipedia.org/wiki/Emotional_intelligence
[xxxi] Roger Connors, Tom Smith, and Craig Hickman, "The Oz Principle: Getting Results Through Individual and Organizational Accountability," Portfolio; Rev Upd edition (May 4, 2010), p. 47
[xxxii] Performance Research Associates, "Delivering Knock Your Socks Off Service" (Paperback), 4th Ed., pp. 9–31
[xxxiii] http://icsatoday.org/about/mission/
[xxxiv] business-ecosystem; https://www.investopedia.com/terms/b/business-ecosystem.asp
[xxxv] Ibid
[xxxvi] https://en.wikipedia.org/wiki/Innovation
[xxxvii] Maria Trimarchi, How the Galapagos Islands Work https://science.howstuffworks.com/life/evolution/galapagos-islands1.htm
[xxxviii] https://en.wikipedia.org/wiki/Innovation
[xxxix] Chris Zach Hidalgo, Definition of integrity; http://www.webweevers.com/integrity.htm Complete article, used with permission. Retrieved Monday, December 16, 2002
[xl] Definition of communication. http://www.merriam-webster.com/dictionary/communication
[xli] James O'Toole, "Leadership A to Z: A Guide for the Appropriately Ambitious", Jossey-Bass Business & Management Series, Hardcover, 1999, p. 43
[xlii] Compiled by The Dialogue Consultants from Thomas Crum, Peter Senge, and Robert Nash
[xliii] Adapted from a paper prepared by Shelley Berman, which was based on discussions of the Dialogue Group of the Boston Chapter of Educators for Social Responsibility (ESR). http://en.copian.ca/library/learning/study/scdvd.htm
[xliv] Peter Spence and Charles Crichton, Video Arts Limited, Northbrook, Ill., Video Arts, ©1986
[xlv] QBQ! The Question Behind the Question: Practicing Personal Accountability at Work and in Life, TarcherPerigee; 1 edition, September 9, 2004, p. 4
[xlvi] Ibid., pp. 100–105
[xlvii] Ibid., p. 10
[xlviii] Ibid., p. 26
[xlix] Ibid., p. 27
[l] Ibid., p. 3
[li] Ibid., p. 43

[lii] Ibid., p. 46
[liii] Ibid., p. 18
[liv] Ibid., p. 10
[lv] Sue Annis Hammond and Andrea B. Mayfield, "The Thin Book Of Naming Elephants: How to Surface Undiscussables for Greater Organizational Success. Or How to STOP investing in our Assumptions," Thin Book Publishing Co., 2004, p. 4
[lvi] Ibid., p. 3
[lvii] Ibid., p. 8
[lviii] Ibid., p. 8
[lix] Ibid., p. 10
[lx] Ibid., p. 9
[lxi] Ibid., p. 10
[lxii] Ibid., p. 12
[lxiii] Ibid., p. 18
[lxiv] Ibid., p. 26
[lxv] Ibid., p. 31
[lxvi] Ibid., p. 32
[lxvii] Ibid., p. 33
[lxviii] Ibid., p. 34
[lxix] Ibid., p. 33
[lxx] Ibid., p. 34
[lxxi] Ibid., p. 41
[lxxii] Ibid., 80; Barry Oshry, Seeing Systems: Unlocking the Mysteries of Organizational Life 2nd Edition; Berrett-Koehler Publishers; 2nd edition (August 12, 2007)
[lxxiii] Sue Annis Hammond and Andrea B. Mayfield, "The Thin Book Of Naming Elephants: How to Surface Undiscussables for Greater Organizational Success. Or How to STOP investing in our Assumptions," Thin Book Publishing Co., 2004, p. 43
[lxxiv] Ibid; Karl E. Weick and Kathleen M. Sutcliffe, <u>Managing The Unexpected: Assuring High Performance In An Age Of Complexity</u>, Jossey-Bass; 1 edition (July 3, 2001)
[lxxv] Ibid., p. 44
[lxxvi] David Cooperrider, "Why Appreciative Inquiry," <u>Lessons from the Field: Applying Appreciative Inquiry</u> (Thin Book Publishing, 2002)
[lxxvii] Sue Annis Hammond and Andrea B. Mayfield, "The Thin Book Of Naming Elephants: How to Surface Undiscussables for Greater Organizational Success. Or How to STOP investing in our Assumptions," Thin Book Publishing Co., 2004, p. 92
[lxxviii] Definition of trust. http://www.merriam-webster.com/dictionary/trust
[lxxix] Rosemary Bryant, How Workplace Culture Can Attract the Right Employees, TriNet Blog, May 17, 2016. http://www.trinet.com/hr-insights/blog/2016/how-workplace-culture-can-attract-the-right-employees
[lxxx] Definition of values. http://www.answers.com/Q/What_is_the_definition_of_Values
[lxxxi] Definition of values. http://encyclopedia.thefreedictionary.com/values
[lxxxii] Michael Josephson, Michael Josephson of the Josephson Institute of Ethics There's No Such Thing as Business Ethics Character Counts Commentary #343:1

[lxxxiii] Hull, Patrick, "Answer 4 Questions to Get a Great Mission Statement," Forbes. Forbes Media, LLC, 10 January 2013
[lxxxiv] Roger Connors, Tom Smith, and Craig Hickman, "The Oz Principle: Getting Results Through Individual and Organizational Accountability," Portfolio; Rev Upd edition, May 4, 2010, p. 47
[lxxxv] Definition of drive http://www.oxforddictionaries.com/us/definition/american_english/drive
[lxxxvi] Definition of integrity. http://www.thefreedictionary.com/integrity
[lxxxvii] Dr. Larry Roper, Relationships: The Critical Ties That Bind Professionals NEW DIRECTIONS FOR STUDENT SERVICES, no. 98, Summer 2002 © Wiley Periodicals, Inc., p. 12
[lxxxviii] Charles Ram Bossidy, "Execution (The Discipline of Getting Things Done)" (Hardcover), Crown Business, NY; Copyright 2002, Larry, p. 22
[lxxxix] Ibid., p. 23
[xc] Ibid., p. 22
[xci] Ibid., p. 32
[xcii] https://www.usatoday.com/story/sports/nfl/2018/09/03/colin-kaepernick-nike-ad-just-do-protest/1186501002/
[xciii] The Death of responsibility. https://www.linkedin.com/pulse/death-responsibility-russell-davis-sphr-shrm-scp/
[xciv] Jacob Burak, "Humans are wired for bad news, angry faces and sad memories. Is this negativity bias useful or something to overcome?," Is Aeon: digital magazine of ideas and culture, 04 September, 2014. https://aeon.co/essays/humans-are-wired-for-negativity-for-good-or-ill
[xcv] Peter H. Diamandis and Steven Kotler, "Abundance: The Future is Better Than You Think," Free Press Hardcover, February 2012, p. IX
[xcvi] Ibid., p. 38
[xcvii] Ibid., p. 38
[xcviii] Ibid., p. 38
[xcix] Definition of commitment. https://www.vocabulary.com/dictionary/commitment
[c] Definition of honesty. http://www.merriam-webster.com/dictionary/honesty
[ci] Definition of openness. https://www.vocabulary.com/dictionary/openness
[cii] Definition of initiative. https://www.seslisozluk.net/en/what-is-the-meaning-of-initiative/
[ciii] Definition of communication. http://www.cbv.ns.ca/bec/cmt/com_meaning.html
[civ] Definition of engagement. http://www.thefreedictionary.com/engagement
[cv] Xuhua Chen, "Memorize SAT Vocabulary The Quantum Way (Volume 1)," August 1, 2012, Xuhua Chen Publisher, p. 291
[cvi] Bella DePaulo Ph.D., Psychology Today, February 2, 2017, https://www.psychologytoday.com/blog/living-single/201702/what-is-the-divorce-rate-really
[cvii] Dr. Larry Roper, Relationships: The Critical Ties That Bind Professionals NEW DIRECTIONS FOR STUDENT SERVICES, no. 98, Summer 2002 © Wiley Periodicals, Inc., p. 15

[cviii] Ibid., p. 12
[cix] Ibid., p. 13
[cx] Ibid., p. 11
[cxi] http://islandconnectionnews.com/op-ed-remove-confederate-flag-from-statehouse-grounds/
[cxii] https://www.washingtonpost.com/politics/courts_law/obamacare-survives-supreme-court-challenge/2015/06/25/af87608e-188a-11e5-93b7-5eddc056ad8a_story.html?noredirect=on&utm_term=.b2025a69e161
[cxiii] https://en.wikipedia.org/wiki/Obergefell_v._Hodges
Obergefell v. Hodges, No. 14-556, slip op. at 22–23 (U.S. June 26, 2015) ("The Court now holds that same-sex couples may exercise the fundamental right to marry. [...] [T]he State laws challenged by Petitioners in these cases are now held invalid to the extent they exclude same-sex couples from civil marriage on the same terms and conditions as opposite-sex couples.")
Denniston, Lyle (June 26, 2015). "Opinion Analysis: Marriage Now Open to Same-Sex Couples". SCOTUSblog. Retrieved July 2, 2015
[cxiv] Definition of teamwork.
http://www.oxforddictionaries.com/us/definition/american_english/teamwork
[cxv] Definition of teamwork.
http://www.businessdictionary.com/definition/teamwork.html
[cxvi] Roger Connors, Tom Smith, and Craig Hickman, "The Oz Principle: Getting Results Through Individual and Organizational Accountability," Portfolio; Rev Upd edition, May 4, 2010, p. 47
[cxvii] http://www.businessdictionary.com/definition/management-by-walking-around-MBWA.html
[cxviii] TheNumber.com; Avengers: Age of Ultron, 2015. http://www.the-numbers.com/movie/Avengers-Age-of-Ultron#tab=summary; © 1997-2016 Nash Information Services, LLC. All rights reserved. The Numbers is a registered trademark of Nash Information Services, LLC
[cxix] Yahoo Sports; The Mayweather-Pacquiao fight shattered expectations, and Mayweather could end up making $250 million.
http://sports.yahoo.com/news/mayweather-pacquiao-fight-shattered-expectations-131130531.html
[cxx] Internal Displacement Monitoring Centre (IDMC), Norwegian Refugee Council, Global Overview 2015. http://www.internal-displacement.org/assets/library/Media/201505-Global-Overview-2015/201505-GO2015-press-release-en.pdf
[cxxi] Police: 101-year-old man rescued one week after Nepal quake
http://www.cnn.com/2015/05/03/asia/nepal-earthquake/index.html © 2016 Cable News Network. Turner Broadcasting System, Inc. All Rights Reserved. CNN Sans ™ & © 2016 Cable News Network
[cxxii] Ibid.
[cxxiii] Adm. McRaven Urges Graduates to Find Courage to Change the World, May 16, 2014; UTNews The University of Texas at Austin

http://news.utexas.edu/2014/05/16/mcraven-urges-graduates-to-find-courage-to-change-the-world
[cxxiv] Ibid.
[cxxv] Ibid.
[cxxvi] Conflict resolution for managers and leaders; The CDR Associates Training Package; Participants Workbook; 2007 by John Wiley & Sons, Inc; pub Josey –Bass, p. 23
[cxxvii] Steve McGuire, The Hidden Cost of Workplace Conflict, January 2014, Mediate.com everything mediation. http://www.mediate.com/articles/McGuireS1.cfm
[cxxviii] How Much Is Conflict Costing You? Including Facts and Figures about the Direct and Hidden Costs of Conflict And A Cost of Conflict Calculation Worksheet July 2007; © 2007 John Ford and Associates, Oakland, California, p. 2. www.johnford.com
[cxxix] Ibid., p. 3
[cxxx] Neil Wagner, Bad Bosses Follow You Home: Having a difficult boss at work strains workers' personal relationships at home. But some relationships are immune, December 21, 2011, The Doctor Will See You Now
http://www.thedoctorwillseeyounow.com/content/emotional_health/art3535.html
[cxxxi] Neil Wagner, Some Bosses Are Bad for Your Health, A new study has found what you may have suspected: The stress of a bad boss can put you at risk for heart disease, December 9, 2008, The Doctor Will See You Now
http://www.thedoctorwillseeyounow.com/content/emotional_health/art3535.html
[cxxxii] Alice G. Walton, The Impact of Bad Bosses, The Atlantic, February 25, 2012. http://www.theatlantic.com/health/archive/2012/02/the-impact-of-bad-bosses/253423/
[cxxxiii] Definition of power. http://www.merriam-webster.com/dictionary/power
[cxxxiv] Mipham J. Mukpo, "Turning the Mind Into An Ally. Riverhead Books," The Berkley Publishing Group, Sakyong Mipham, 2003, p. 197
[cxxxv] Ibid., p. 199
[cxxxvi] Definition of perspective. http://www.merriam-webster.com/dictionary/perspective
[cxxxvii] Definition of perseverance. http://www.thefreedictionary.com/perseverance
[cxxxviii] http://www.merriam-webster.com/dictionary/leadership

www.ingramcontent.com/pod-product-compliance
Lightning Source LLC
Chambersburg PA
CBHW031619210526
45464CB00004B/1647